GEOGRAPHY

art / race / exile

RALPH LEMON

Performance Text by Tracie Morris

Afterword by Ann Daly

WESLEYAN UNIVERSITY PRESS

Published by University Press of New England   Hanover and London

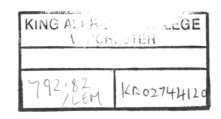
Wesleyan University Press

Published by University Press of New England,

Hanover, NH 03755

© 2000 by Ralph Lemon

Text on pages 167-177 © Tracie Morris

Afterword © 2000 by Ann Daly

Printed in China

5 4 3 2 1

All drawings and photographs are by Ralph Lemon, with the exception of the nine performance photographs at the back of the book, which are © by T. Charles Erickson and used with his permission.

Geography, a project of Cross Performance Inc., was commissioned by Yale Repertory Theatre in cooperation with 651 ARTS and the National Dance Project, a project of the New England Foundation for the Arts with support from the National Endowment for the Arts, the Andrew W. Mellon Foundation, the John S. and James L. Knight Foundation, and Philip Morris Companies Inc. *Geography* was also funded by Africa Exchange, an international program of 651 ARTS supported by a grant from the Ford Foundation; and by the Rockefeller Foundation's Multi-Arts Production Fund. Support for the artistic development of *Geography* was also provided by Metropolitan Life Foundation. *Geography* was a part of the Philip Morris New Works Fund, sponsored by Philip Morris Companies Inc.

The ninety-minute performance directed and choreographed by Ralph Lemon featured a cast of nine men of African descent from Côte d'Ivoire, Guinea, and the United States. It premiered in October 1997 at Yale Repertory Theatre, New Haven, Connecticut, and toured to Walker Art Center, Minneapolis, Minnesota; Duke University Institute of the Arts, Durham, North Carolina; University of Texas, Austin; and 651 ARTS and the Brooklyn Academy of Music, New York.

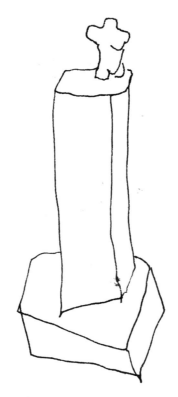

returning from the strangeness
of the soul school's language
I am in love more than ever

Preface

This first part begins in 1989 and quickly and without historical sequence jumps to 1995, when I first met Zao, who said that I just needed to relax.

GEOGRAPHY

I have always
wanted to go
to New Guinea

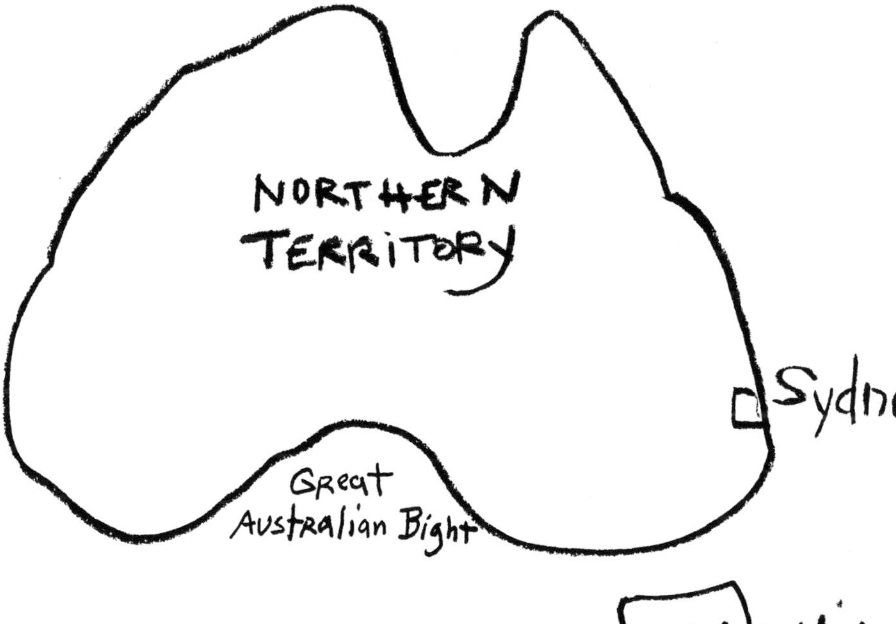

In Australia in 1989.
watching two aboriginal dancers
teach a group of dancers who
were not aboriginal, but
who were eager to learn.
The small blue black man
and woman crouched,
sheltered in a corner
of the studio

in downtown Sydney, far from
their private northern landscape,
communicating in complete silence
until it was time for them
to teach their dance. He
wore blue jeans and a brown
T-shirt. She wore a sleeveless
yellow dress. I had never
seen a body become what

it was pretending to be.
I think that it was a
Kangaroo dance. I thought
that I would like to move
like that.

WHY I CHOSE THE WORD GEOGRAPHY

In the early spring of '96, Sam Miller and Cynthia Mayeda, two dance saints, called and asked if I would like to do a project at Yale Repertory Theatre. I had just disbanded the straight legs, elongated spines, and pointed feet of my modern dance company and at the moment had terrible stage fright. Sam asked if I could catch a train to New Haven that next day to talk to Stan Wojewodski about what I might do in his theater. Stan and I were strangers, and I could only imagine that for some reason he felt compelled to disrupt his more certain Rep schedule. I tried to come up with an excuse to make my availability more complicated but thought that this might be an opportunity to challenge whatever discrepancy I now projected. On the train I wrote on a piece of paper what I might do. I had recently returned from Haiti, where I found myself inventing Africa. I then heard that there was to be a West Africa Inroads conference in New York City, a conference about West African dance, music, and theater. I had not been to Africa before this project and—unlike the "invisible" Haiti island off the coast of Florida, or far far away Australia—Africa has always been a source of proximal emotional challenges. Africa is not Haiti, and Africa is not Australia, but the whole of Africa is as black as those two aboriginal dancers, which was really the point. Africa would become the source of my finding a new relationship to the stage. Stan liked the idea. I met with Mikki Shepard, the host of this West African performance conference at 651. She helped me board a plane three months later.

After two trips to the Ivory Coast and Ghana, and a year of planning and devising with Tracie Morris, Nari Ward, Stan Pressner, Francisco Lopez, Paul Miller, and Liz Prince, my immensely talented collaborators, Djédjé, Angelo, Nai, Tapé, Goulei, and James arrived. Moussa, originally from Guinea, and Carlos, joined us from their American homes. There were three months of ten-hour days, and six-day weeks of actual physical building, half of that time spent trying to translate what it was we wanted to communicate and discovering that some things simply do not matter. Three months was a ridiculously short amount of time for the communicative cultural possibilities we uncovered, but we were all pleased that we had even a single day's attempt at understanding how we are different and the same.

The performance itself, the theater, what was seen, was simply the discoveries that were made about a limited, contrived community in a context of empirical performance formalism. What is that, you ask? On some level I felt obliged to make art. Beyond that attempt is the truth of trying to understand something other than what I have known. Geography/Africa was in part a performance, but it was equally an anthropological collaboration about being American, African, brown, black, blue black, male, and artist.

HAITI:
THE SECOND TIME THAT I HAD SEEN REAL BLACK PEOPLE

A TRUE STORY ABOUT COMING TO AMERICA AS TOLD BY STEPHEN SENATUS

1. I wanted to travel. I saw everybody leaving. I got up and left.

2. The boat was too full. Some were thrown over, and some jumped themselves.

3. I don't know when I disembarked. I don't know what happened, because they killed me and threw me overboard.

4. I fell asleep. I don't know what happened. I didn't know if they had come or not. When I regained consciousness I found myself naked like my mother made me. All my body was burned and bruised.

5. And then a single hand, like this, my hand, that was what it was like. It picked me up like a little pile of garbage. It walked with me through the grove and dropped me against a wall. I stood on my two legs. I walked and walked. I found a house and found all the people I saw on the boat, and they said, "There is Stephen that died."

HAITIAN JOURNAL

The hero
Zao led us to a nearby driveway or alley or courtyard or maybe simply the extension of the ragged road. Where drums waited. The neighborhood was expectant. Men, women, and children flowed out of their homes and into the street. Bringing light, candle fire. A Vodou-sing along. Little boys mastering and practicing dances while their fathers sang to private Hispaniola constellations, mouths driveling with rum. Mothers and daughters observed from the periphery, boldly smiling, moving quietly. First night in Port-au-Prince.

Second night in Port-au-Prince
Immure. Wide awake, blanketed on the floor of a small, makeshift music studio. A radio blasting from the paper thin wall of the next door family, communal. No air, no cool. No running water. Oswald, my floormate, guide, snoring. DañEl, another floormate, was sick all the night, making water noises on the waterless toilet. The women here have their say at 5:00 A.M. Early church singing. And then another whiff of the very human air entering through the only ventilation, the cracks and crevices of the door. Our host is gracious, a big heart, a musician and political activist, a good man. I cannot spend another evening on the hard surface of his floor. DañEl agrees. We move to a suspect hotel.

Hotel La Palace
Vast and empty. Across the avenue from the president's palace. The electricity and water occasionally disappear. There is a swimming pool, constantly hosed and murky still. No one swims; instead, the water is used by maids to clean the rooms. Carried from pool to room in white plastic lard containers.
More of the tragic decay that was once another opulent untaught playground for tourists, the sophisticated kind, "In the day," before one of many Armageddons.
Kitchens: modern caves of the home. No natural light to see other than the fire on the floor, boiling away whatever stew.
We ate dinner on the wide balcony, overlooking mostly walking, slowly, long brown bodies deserted, but dressed with stained ancient dignity. A few cars, crowded jeeps and the occasional U.N. vehicle.
Thomas, a retired career serviceman joined us for dinner, the only other quest. He has been retired and traveling since 1972, since the age of thirty-seven. He is sixty. He travels wherever exists a U.S. base. He will vote for Colin Powell if he runs. "Why the hell not. And so what if it doesn't work? I've been voting for white people for my

entire life and things have always been fucked-up."

He also likes prostitutes, delivered to him daily, bi-daily. Another older black gentleman preoccupied with fucking exotic black women. The second one I had met in less than a month. The first was a taxi driver in New York City who went on and on about the dark women of Brazil.

Saturday

Zao was scheduled to do a session at one of the two recording studios in Port-au-Prince, in a common cinderblock dwelling housing ancient sound equipment. The session was scheduled for 12:00 P.M.; no one showed. It was rescheduled for 7:00 P.M.; no one showed. At 8:00 Zao had a gig with his band. And then the electricity went out all over the city except for the president's palace (Aristede was not around to feel privileged). At 10:00 the electricity returned.

Zao's "Roots" music gig was at once strange and exciting, Haitian drumming and electric guitars. A concrete stage, outside. The audience sat far away, still, very still, in school desks, set up specifically for the event. None of them dancing; instead, they sat and sipped on soda and ate exotic fried food on plastic plates, making good use of the desks. Onstage, crowded around the band, an entourage of young men dancing and singing in a space, three feet by three feet, reserved for them.

After a deeply emotional set by Zao and his band and entourage and after no great response by the (classroom) audience, a comedian took the stage. Manipulating the natural cadence of Creole, abrupt virtuosic pauses, all rhythm, like a politician. The audience laughed and laughed.

November 4, 1995

After many days in the broken heart of Port-au-Prince we escaped with a three-hour drive to the north in a privately rented tap-tap, destination, Lakou Soukri Danche. The countryside of Haiti's east coast is lush and desert divided. The sun is not as confused, and always threatening.

We passed many small towns, lingering barely minutes. The town before the lakou is Gonaïves, a bigger town than most. We reached Gonaïves as the sun was going down and found a restaurant offering only spaghetti and lambi. When we finished eating, it was twilight. DañEl bought rum for the road. We took turns using the one and only toilet in an empty rental room up above the restaurant.

Once we were back on the road, it became clear that neither our driver nor Oswald, who had been to this place, knew the precise location of the lakou. The road was thick with walkers drenched in night light, and all of them had some things on their backs and a different argument and direction for the lakou's whereabouts.

After another hour of halted but sincere guidance, we found the exact backroad and our post-African paradise. Even in the dark this place seemed to be from another time. The air was simple here, a welcome respite from Port-au-Prince, or anywhere. As we got out of our rented tap-tap we were greeted by a perfect looking old black man, a long frail man with beautiful eyes, skin, and hat. He grabbed my hand and held it as if I were someone he had known and not seen for a long time. The boy children gathering around were wide-eyed, and briefly singing. They led us through the shadows of their temple and farm and the hidden faces and laughter of women to the Mapou tree and to the lake of the spirit *Mau b Inan* (Oswald's translation) where we were invited to wash our hair. On the way back to where we started we were encouraged to pick small produce from radiant moon blue plants. The small boys put more in my pockets.

And then, in light, ascending voices, they asked for money.

By the time that we had all returned to the tap-tap, we and it were covered with a sudden unfamiliar violence, screaming and pulling at backpacks and watches. I was caught outside the vehicle and held onto my bag, shocked within the Creole din. One of the young boys looked me in the eye, put his finger to his neck, and demonstrated how a throat might be quickly sliced opened. I saw no knives. Our driver pushed me into the back of the tap-tap, into the arms and hands of Oswald and DañEl and wildly drove off. Those bodies still hanging on to whatever was protruding from the truck, became dangling, flying silhouettes with free palms outstretched.

Crouched inside the vehicle and bouncing to the rough and rapid getaway, Oswald explained to me that most of the translatable commotion was over who got the obligatory few pennies for the tour, an older teenage spokesman or a younger boy. The beautiful old man was nowhere in sight. (One can't disrupt progress.) And then, none of them were visible. I rode the three-hour ride home with my head in my hands. Oswald fell asleep. DañEl drank his rum and railed on about the federal or national government of America and George Washington's military coup, the unrecorded, other historical sixteen years before his and our country's first election. The remaining ride and road littered with celebration, coming out of nowhere.

Sunday 5

Thomas announced that he was on his third prostitute in less than twenty-four hours. He is leaving Haiti soon and is in a hurry. The third prostitute brought her young daughter along. The twelve-year-old waited alone on the hotel balcony, all dressed in ruffled Sunday white. She posed; I took a photograph of her; the pimp appeared; I photographed him, and then paid them both.

Notes

Looking at the moist skin of these blacks, I need to comprehend some layer of waterless grime, I think, because there is so much poverty here, but it is only sweat. And ultimately my disease.

Men: Misplaced, sit and "hang." No longer have a place or definition of role. Perhaps. Cultural gender displacement. Perhaps.

Women: Work nonstop.

Rules exist unless they have to be broken—mostly broken.

Communal living still. But because now is "modern," better off in the country. Neo Maroons. Perhaps.

This country will survive of course. But to what? Zao will keep making music.

MEMORY DRAWINGS

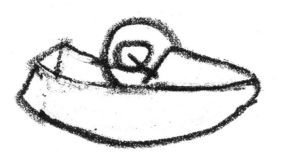

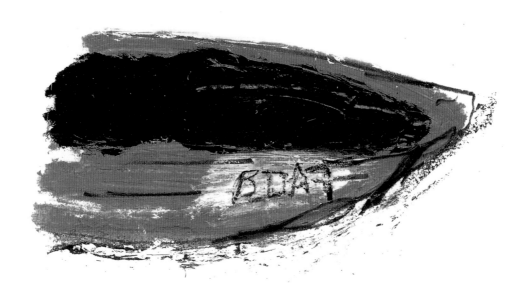

chicken walking down the street in Haiti - Port Au Prince

Faucet in Zao's backyard – Port Au Prince

WHAT I WROTE ON A PIECE OF PAPER ON THE TRAIN TO NEW HAVEN

In this project I will explore the relationship between the postmodern formal concerns of my more recent dancemaking and the performance and dancing of traditional Haitian and West African dance and theater. (The terms "traditional," "Haitian" and "West African" are presented here very generally and only represent a starting point in my search for specificity.) Basically, I will create a work of theater, dance, and music that intersects the performance boundaries of multiple and very different worlds. I will also explore the perceptions of racial and cultural identities, and how an identity is translated, divided, subsumed and empowered by another culturally foreign and directive aesthetic.

As an African American removed from any obvious African culture by many generations, I find in this project an opportunity to spiral to some commonality —an intersection of my life and work with that of a subjectively perceived (perhaps romanticized), original source experience of African dancing and performing. In concept, these foreign artists bring to my modernism an almost inscrutable sense of purpose, a mysterious insight into the tradition of Pan-African dance and theater. I hope to break down these myths in my own aesthetic to find a language that brings this working group to a place that is not romanticized or overtly exotic but that is genuine and new in its form. I then can offer a useful connected point of view from the nonlinear passage of a tradition that has traveled from Africa to Haiti to my art culture.

I will direct this work in deference to the traditions of these African and Haitian performers. These performers will bring an unfamiliar process to my world, thereby challenging and demanding change of my self-imposed and limited physical language. And I will bring to their world an American formalism that respectfully manipulates their traditional environment to a new form of performance. We will workshop our sensibilities to find a voice that creates a new language, one that heightens and disguises the apparent bond of color of skin and the obvious fact that we all dance and speak.

In this work I will work with a number of collaborators. Tracie Morris, one of the most exciting poets writing in the United States today, is a great candidate for text. I will collaborate the singing and drumming of the performers with a yet-to-be named composer who will create a connective sound score (Francisco López, a biologist and sound composer from Spain is a possibility). I will work with a yet-to-be named set and costume designer. And I will work with my longtime lighting designer and collaborator, Stan Pressner.

There are two possible versions of this work. One would be a smaller-cast version with three performers; two Haitian dancers/musicians and myself. These Haitian performers live in Miami and their proximity and availability would make workshopping somewhat simple. The other version would incorporate the two Haitian performers and eight performers from West Africa. This version would require an extensive research period; also, to bring these artists to this country for an extended time would be complicated. (Among broader investigations I have an immediate plan to travel to the Ivory Coast in August, and I have a contact there who will set up an interview for me with the Ballet National de la Côte d'Ivoire.) The production elements would be relative to the time and scale of the two versions. There is also the option that the first version is a workshop version, an opportunity to investigate the larger work.

March 20, 1996

But then there was a problem with the Haitians. One Haitian artist could not make himself available: "I cannot commit to such a long project because I don't even know where I will be tomorrow." He eventually went back to Haiti to live in the mountains for six months, to be with the spirits. The other artist literally disappeared; none of his friends knew where he was. Later someone said that he thought he saw him walking down a street in Boston. What a beautiful dancer he is.
Now there was no island between Africa and myself.

GEOGRAPHY

AUGUST 1996

ABIDJAN: THROUGH THE EYES OF SOMEONE WHO SHOULD KNOW BETTER

The airport is smaller than I expected, made even smaller by the many boys hustling for bags. In their rough T-shirts they seem hungry and then proud. It is at first a frightful city. The space here, the air and light, has the option of neutralizing the desperation to my eyes, and sometimes it does. Everywhere the women are radiantly dressed in endless cloth, most are growing small babies on their backs.

From our hotel balcony you can see the Treichville bridge, which we are advised not to walk across day or night. There are many people who walk across the bridge all the time. Across the bridge, at the Treichville Market, the women are an ocean of improvised fabric, grains, and red meat, and only seem interested in my eating from their dirty hands. I feel oddly safe with most of the thin, conniving men who ultimately just want to show their teeth and bargain for time.

Thursday is an unnamed holiday, open only to Cathédrale St-Paul, which lies on the northern fringe of Le Plateau. Hard-featured and demanding. So we sit in its oceanic pews, watching a young boy sweeping the whole of the space with a simple twig. Two young men sit behind us, holding hands. Brothers, friends hold hands, I am told.

All the while I try to contact Souleymane Koly of the Ensemble Koteba with a phone that will not accept my apparitional French. Among the Baoulé, Bété, and Gouro of Adidjan I am looking for Lobi-figured men who drum and dance. Maybe I am too far south for my little ancestral experiment.

At the American Embassy there is a man behind a thick pane of glass who warns about the violence throughout the whole of the country. How even a family of missionaries in the north were robbed in their home at riflepoint. I do not see it— solemnity, anger perhaps, but not what I would call violence.

Within the compound of the home of the choreographer of the Ensemble Koteba there is a low brick dwelling. In its backyard is a thatched roof that religiously covers a concrete floor. Five young women sing in its center. Theirs are voices from a preternatural system. There was also a woman there from Paris or Belgium, a guest, who was giving voice lessons or some kind of New World theatrical instruction, intrusively. She wanted them to sway while singing and to bring more volume to their songs. Slowly, they watched her suggesting gestures, respectful, and responded by singing what I would consider perfectly anomalous songs slightly beyond whispers.

When speaking and eating, prehistory still survives within the country's fading French prettiness. The very poor and the maquis keep all the old secrets.

From the balcony of our hotel, this morning, the first thing that I see when I wake up is a young boy carrying pillows to sell. He stops alongside the road to shit. Once I was told that the African eats with his right hand and wipes himself with his left, a story from a Chinese sailor turned New York dishwasher. To the side of the balcony a man rolls in the grass completely naked. I play one of my favorite travel games and imagine no modern architecture surrounding his flailing body. Otherwise this morning is the same.

We took a long taxi ride to the Adjamé bus station to buy tickets to Korhogo and met the complex event of older boys, potential guides, pulling the taxi apart. I refused our exit and we drove on. This was our first experience of danger here, so far, more heroic than Port-au-Prince but like a twin. Stuck in Abidjan, a city, not West Africa, or, all that West Africa is today.

Dimanche. Rain. August 18. A new bed. The room is smaller than the room in Abidjan proper. There is no seat on the toilet. The room across from ours has a television blaring the entire time of its nearness. Palms surround the hotel. A dirt road of red earth marks its place in this history. There is new singing in the background, somewhere. It turns out to be another television.

We enter the Ki-Yi Villa of Werewere Liking, my second arranged contact. Today there is a baptism for a newborn, escargot and plantains, and dancing to Michael Jackson. One young man was dressed for a northern U.S. winter, complete with ski boots. There are castaways here celebrating their freedom, mostly girls, given away by their Muslim fathers. On all other days everyone practices ancient performing forms from dawn to dusk.

Postcard: Not a vacation but perhaps a sensory holiday where the environs are in total control of what you see, feel, eat, speak or not, plus what comes later.

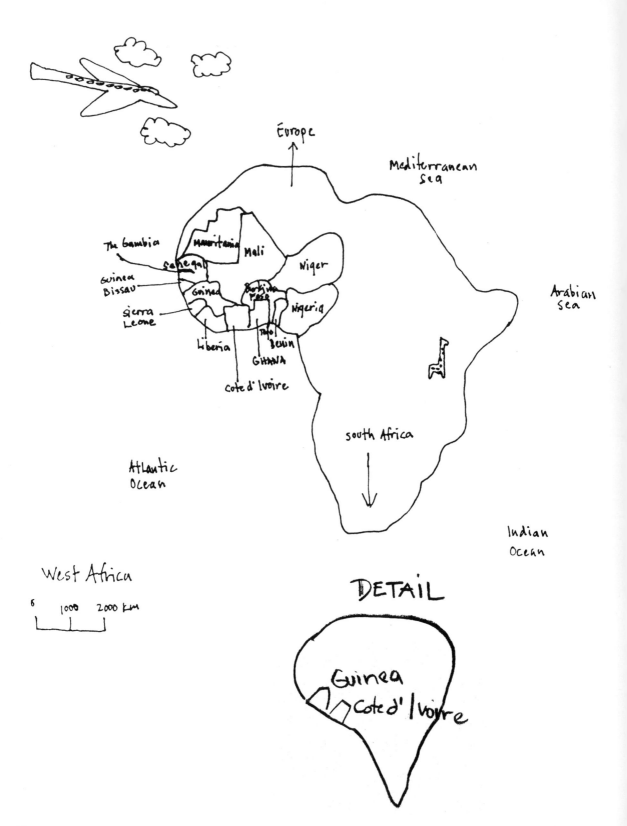

Europe

Mediterranean Sea

The Gambia

Mauritania   Mali

Senegal   Niger

Guinea Bissau

Guinea   Burkina Faso   Arabian Sea

Sierra Leone   Nigeria

Liberia   Togo   Benin

GHANA

Cote d' Ivoire

south Africa

Atlantic Ocean

Indian Ocean

West Africa

6   1000   2000 km

DETAIL

Guinea   Cote d' Ivoire

28

We visit Cocody's jungle suburbia. The market here is manicured, empty. The merchants are aggressive, more than in Treichville. A tall man approaches and speaks a sparse brand of English. His name is Pierre and he is from Senegal. At first he tries to sell us some malachite and then he offers tea. I am not sure what he means. In a need to decipher his offer and in a broader plan to feel ordinary, we accept. Along the circuitous walk to a housing complex, similar to any common ghetto in America, I imagine being led to a trap, soured bodies too close, guns, and a robbery. We reach our destination and enter a lovely apartment flooded with sunlight. There are books on the art of Côte d'Ivoire, pictures of Pierre on holiday with a smiling blond girlfriend, stunted talk of the world, and there is tea, Senegalese style, three cups, each serving prepared in ritual.

Monday is a day of practice at the Ki-Yi Villa. I photograph a row of orphans and sons and daughters sitting on a long low broken wall, drumming in dying sunlight. I watch two acrobats somersault onto ungiving concrete, again and again. The drumming continues as I fall asleep.

Ensemble Koteba rehearses not at a villa but today at the Centre Culturel Français. Only the men; the women are all attending a wedding so there is very little singing. It is a work about the hunting tradition of Mali. I don't know the title of this work but it is the work of Souleymane Koly, who directs the ensemble. Souleymane says that there is an American in Mali who is going through an initiation to become a traditional Malian hunter. It will take the rest of his life. As I watch these performers, it is entertaining experiencing what my looking translates and what it does not. When they are finished I think that all that I can judge is anatomic alertness. Souleymane asks if I can come tomorrow to see the whole production. Tomorrow we leave for Ghana.

Before I came to Africa an African acquaintance who lives in Brooklyn told me that Souleymane is from Guinea and that Guinea and Côte d'Ivoire are the same, the same people. I was also told that Mali is "authentic," Côte d'Ivoire is not really, and that there is no longer an Ivory Coast. "Côte d'Ivoire" is now the official name in all languages. There is not a similar name problem with any other French-speaking African country, although the French pronunciation of "Niger" is a challenge. I have always been fascinated with the chronological sequence of the names "Niger" and "Nigeria" or was it "Nigeria" and then "Niger"? I have been to neither place. And never have I been around so many poor black people and not heard the word "nigger."

The Ghana–Côte d'Ivoire frontier: Hours and hours spent watching and waiting. It is almost 3:00 P.M. We have traveled only a few kilometers. I forgot my vaccination document in Abidjan. It is not much of a problem. With the help of a very friendly Ghanaian I was issued another after paying out 4000 CFAs. I met a man who travels with an expired passport, simply by paying more to the police and military for his passage. He was very proud of this regulation.

GHANA

At Takoradi we took a bush taxi to Kumasi. (The British originally spelled it Kummassi. During that original time the British had African officers but would not let them wear shoes.) A four and a half hour ride through forest, bush, and jungle at about seventy mph. I see no animals. Packed like a conjoined community, the taxi occupants sleep. Their heads are bowed forward, resting on the most available surface, in an ancient travel prayer.

The rest of the day was spent being a tourist: the Fort Kumasi military museum; two markets, buying old necklaces and older carvings; and Adehyeman Gardens, a popular Ghanaian restaurant that had no electricity and no faces, dark hands, dark fufu, and ginger wine. Tonight we are all laughing.

In Ghana some speak a mix of "Twi" and English. In South Carolina where my mother was born there is no similar sound. Most Ghanaians refer to me as a white man. I asked one man why and his reply was, "Because you are, because you are not from Africa."

Hank Williams's "I'm So Lonesome I Could Die" is playing on the bus radio. It is Friday morning. We have been at this bus station since 6:45 A.M.; it is now 10:15. A taxi driver from the night before woke us up at 6:00 to rush us off to the bus station. The bus finally takes off at 10:20. It is not completely full, which should make the trip more pleasant. Patsy Kline sings of crazy arms. Blue-black women adjust their headwraps. Children here barely cry. The bus stops again at 10:23. I suppose the driver needs to pick up his lunch or try to remember where he and we are going. One lone man gets on. A medium part of the bus has to readjust. Following the man, three women, as sparkling draped whales, expand the aisle. And then a group of plainer men. The bus is now full. Glen Campbell is singing "Dream, Dream, Dream" by the Everly Brothers. I would like to hear his "Galveston." I cannot imagine these local people living where this music is made. Yesterday we hired a guide and his two friends. He said his name was Joseph. Joseph is fifteen and seemed to be dying from the physical demand of someone five times his age. He told us that he has had malaria five times. He took us back to the market, where we all got too much sun. We bought them wallets and groceries: bread, crackers, butter, and condensed milk. In every other sentence Joseph would say, "Oh, I am so happy to see you." During the rest of the year he said that he attends some kind of school. Now he is on the street and slightly falling apart or starving. At 10:45 the bus takes off again.

Abidjan

Final images: 1. An old man, thin, slightly bent. His two hands, arms holding an antique transistor radio, its long antennae guiding his front. 2. A place on a street corner for crippled boys. One has no use of his legs. His pelvis is frozen, peaking the pyramid of his dead legs and sloping spine. His arms and sandaled hands support his movement and begging. 3. The act of impasse. Police, military, a larger body, a smaller body, stalling in tight uniforms. 4. Squatting in an inch of urine, in a cinderblock square covering, orchestrated by a thousand flies. 5. The Villa gives a performance on the last night of our trip. The dancing and singing and drumming are stripped down and very complex; the last vital, desperate breathing of functional starvation. Also, men with hair growing and adorned as if peacocks could grow horns. I am inspired.

Seven hundred eighty-three miles from New York. Throughout the flight there are short silent films on Africa. Tourist commercials. In the films everyone is presentable, bright. The backgrounds are carefully edited and the time of a given image in no way conveys how long it takes for all of nothing to happen.

NOVEMBER 1996

QUESTIONS FROM TRACIE MORRIS FOR RALPH

Ralph: If there is an accusation toward your form of African American
dance/art, where does it come from?
Where is the harmony in your conflict?
How do you maintain your African American culture?
How/why did you make the choice to do this "other" work, outside of your
perceived past experiences?
Where is the loyalty of your choices?

DECEMBER 3, 1996

A PARTIAL AUTOBIOGRAPHY ABOUT RACE AND ART: A
LETTER TO TRACIE MORRIS: MOST OF THIS IS TRUE
(UPDATED VERSION)

I was born in Cincinnati, Ohio. That had been the extent of my family's particular
journey north. My family was otherwise from South Carolina and Georgia and very
mixed in the colors of their skin. My mother, her mother, my grandfather, my great-
grandfather were all white, actually off-white, as far as my eyes could see. Irish and
French pigment ratios overpowering what were also West African and Cherokee.
Some of them passed as white, sitting in the front of buses, cream-colored straw hats
and all, when that was an appropriate thing to do. I later grew up in Minneapolis,
Minnesota, and grew to disown Cincinnati, the last city where I remember myself as a
Negro. My father, his work, and family were transferred to Minnesota in the spring of
1963. It was here that I heard "nigger" for the first time. In the beginning most of my
friends in Minneapolis were black, four neighborhood blocks full inside a white
friendly primacy of snow. I loved Minneapolis. And I liked my fewer white friends as
much as I did my black friends except for the six months that I was a member of the
Washburn High School Afro-American Student Union. My parents made me quit
after one of the members, who was also a member of the Black Panther Party, blew
himself up while carrying some kind of bomb through a nearby neighborhood at
three o'clock one April morning. It was also during this time that I helped beat up
one of my best white friends, because he was white and because Martin Luther King
had been assassinated the day before. A little gang of us, theoretically upset. My
punches and kicks were well acted. I apologized later, but only with my eyes. Our

friendship ended; neither of us made that choice. After high school I went to the University of Minnesota and lost touch with most of my black friends. Some of them did not graduate from high school; some were married right after high school and then got jobs; one or two died accidentally or committed suicide. I continued to listen to black music. My mother hated Minneapolis. At her job some of the white men that she would serve coffee to would say to her that they liked their coffee like they liked their women, "black and sweet." She would often come home in tears. I suppose that an adult could tell that my mother was not white. When it was possible for her to move back down south she did. All of my family did, except me; the year was 1971. Most of the women in my life, while I was growing up, were white of skin, or white enough. The young girl in Cincinnati who first broke my heart was black, dark. Twenty years ago Nancy Hauser was alive and white. Nancy danced with Hanya Holm who danced in Germany in the 1930s. Nancy Hauser was my first dance teacher and mentor. I can't imagine having had the same unthreatening art experience if Nancy had been a black male, like my dark-skinned father, whom I loved and feared, whose color variation my variation favors, or like my male distant

cousins who were like some of the scary kids in our quietly segregated neighborhood in Cincinnati. But not like my older brother, who was my first hero and whose hair is like mine but whose skin color is like my mother's. Meredith Monk was also truly white but also Jewish and another art mentor. More than that, because her work was remarkably more than I could comprehend. She said that I danced like an Alvin Ailey

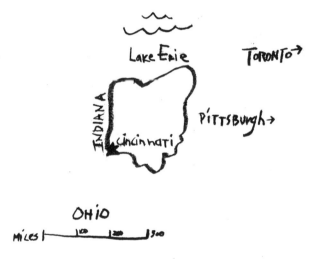

dancer. I found this statement confusing, but since she was a *genius* I didn't dispute her. She didn't actually think this but a friend of hers told her that she thought so. I never studied with Alvin Ailey but met him once a couple of years before he died. I introduced myself but he didn't say hello and immediately began to talk. He said that he was very poor and sad and that his company was very important in spite of his poverty and sadness. I thought that he was a very handsome man. Elaborating, Meredith went on to tell me that my dance technique, my training, whatever it was, had robbed me of my "true soul." I didn't respond. By this time I watched and lived a

a civil rights man taking a nap

New York City "downtown" art scene. It was a white world with a handful of black artists who did not seem to care where and what they were. Or, there was a general feeling of privilege in being part of this environment. Furthermore, they did not seem out of place. The black artists in this world seemed to get as much support and encouragement as the whites. At least their art seemed as adventurous. I say this in retrospect; at the time I don't think that I saw color as much as I saw opportunity. My ex-wife is white and she helped me start my first dance company. By this time most of my close friends in New York were white, except for one or two blacks, one of whom was a beautiful man from the Caribbean who danced with me for a while. The other was a black woman, a beautiful dancer from Michigan and in a relationship with a woman from Brazil. Otherwise, for the next ten years, my company was all white except for me. Once, during this ten-year period a dance critic made a reference to the racial make up of my company. How I was black and had an all-white company and how much they liked the work anyway. Post-Ailey companies, some named after particular cities in the United States seemed to be the real enemy. The artistic director of one of them once told a reporter that she would not let her company see my work because she did not want them to be influenced. She was later relieved and amused when some from her group did see my work and hated it. Once in a small New England college I watched Talley Beatty (a contemporary of Alvin Ailey) walk out of a performance of my work. Later I heard that he thought that he was going to see some "black dance." I was never invited to any of the black dance conferences that meet annually. To this day I have not been to one and don't know what they do there. I suppose I am not considered a "black dance artist." This is not painful; mostly it's hearsay. Much of the conflict part I've probably made up, but I do feel slightly insulted. Before now I don't think that I would ever have found the time to travel to one of these events anyway, but now I would probably go if asked. I was always quite satisfied doing all that I was doing as a dance artist. It felt completely natural from beginning to end. I was never confused. As long as I was walled inside a studio or on a stage, performing to shadows, there was equilibrium. Recently I heard that there is so much tension in this genre issue because the generations of black dance artists right after Ailey (who by the way are mostly black women) feel abandoned in their art-politic purpose by younger black artists like me. My loyalty is in question. They had a difficult, nearly impossible time growing up as black women and then as artists. None of the white companies would hire them as dancers, so they created their own studios, using Ailey as a mentor. I can understand why I would be a threat, but then, their experience is not mine. And that I lack their experience is perhaps why I am also threatened by them. Recently, and after many of my earlier racial nonthoughts had changed their matter, a woman, white, on my board of

This script is divided into two main parts with subdivisions.

The concept begins with personally proposed cultural collisions within the African-based Diaspora (largely autobiographical) and attempts to formally impose an outline narrative of Aeschylus's *The Oresteia* (the Robert Fagles translation). (This compositional idea was inspired by Pier Paolo Passolini's film study *African Orestes*. A study for a film, that was never made and that positioned postcolonial Africa as a backdrop to the Orestes myth.)

The *Oresteia* is said to be an initiation into culture. How a culture ridden by guilt achieves greatness, honesty. In the *Oresteia* there is a gradual climb from torment, through testing, into light—but darkness breeds the light. It is a passion, a tragedy, and a play of restoration.

I use the whole *Oresteia* as an invisible narrative element, not for the eyes of an audience, but to guide and give a Western epic score to my more important concerns with African and African American unity and disunity in art and physical performance politics. To the specific Orestes character I bring some relevant autobiography. I shall work with extremes—the tradition of humanistic representation, and the formalism of abstract fundamentals. I hope to create a balance between the exaggerations, an interdependence, an adaptation. (On a more basic level I shall explore the perceived notion of "the eloquence of black body language," and the long tradition of racist "Western ambivalence towards the 'black primitive,' who can be culturally retrograde, temperamentally mysterious, and physically appealing all at the same time" (*Darwin's Athletes* by John Hoberman).

The actual *Oresteia* consists of three plays: *Agamemnon*, *The Libation Bearers*, and *The Eumenides*. I have broken the last play, *The Eumenides*, into two parts and I have given the proposed *Geography* translation of each play a working title: Map, Crime, Trial, and Divination. This draft, of course, is just words (play and prospects) and its intent is only to guide the work to a more directly relevant experience, language, and collaboration.

> *I* Agamemnon/*Map*
> *The* Oresteia *begins with the fall of Troy. Its propelling force is the murder of Agamemnon by his queen, Clytemnestra, in part because he had earlier sacrificed their daughter Iphigeneia "to charm away the savage winds of Thrace," a possible defeat in war. (As a final insult to Clytemnestra,*

Agamemnon abducted Cassandra from Troy and made her his mistress.) And finally because of the "dark ancestry of Agamemnon's fate."

To this tale I emotionally and imaginatively refer to my father's sacrifice of his post-African–based southern United States experience to the Scandinavian-American environment of Minnesota, a move made to create a better opportunity for our family. That environment greatly informed my aesthetic preferences (Here I must mention that no character in the *Oresteia* is in direct control of any event that each experiences or enacts. It is all "ancestry" and the gods.)

Agamemnon/Map is my history, my unconscious. In the trilogy Orestes is in exile in Agamemnon. Agamemnon/Map also represents the "accusation" from outside by those who feel somewhat betrayed by my choice of art politics and the experiences that created that sensibility. (In a sense, this accusation is a murder of my father, his almost choiceless action to move away from the "Negro"-based environment of Cincinnati, Ohio, in the early 1960s.) Africa (the performers' presence), here, represents a partial, larger unconscious and ancestry.

II The Libation Bearers/*Crime*
Orestes comes home from exile and commits the matricide of Clytemnestra. It is a recrimination for the murder of his father. "The plunge out of darkness into light—the disaster that plunges us into darkness again."

Here I commit the crime of betrayal. A betrayal of the American black dance artworld and possibly the whole continent of Africa, in that I have not literally acknowledged that proposed and complexly defined tradition, as an artist, up to this period in my work. Up to this point, Africa has not had an actual vocal opinion in my work. It will now have that opportunity.

My crime is my acting on my history. My murder is the murder of my African heritage, and of the black dance tradition in America, which feels betrayed and which, perhaps, possesses a defined social and aesthetic connection to an African tradition. This is an exaggerated but possible accusation.
A question: How does the African traditional artist connect to the work of the so-called black American dance/art tradition?

III The Eumenides/*Trial*
In The Eumenides *Orestes is pursued by the Furies, a feminine power that*

must retaliate for the matricide that he has committed. There is the higher intervention by Apollo and Athena. There is the trial where Orestes is judged of his actions. Were they justified or not? The jury is split and Athena casts her vote for Orestes, breaking the split. That vote also represents the new domination of the male psyche in Greek mythology. Orestes is justified and free. "Overcoming the furies with the arrows of Apollo," The Eumenides "sweeps us through light and dark until the light brings forth the torches of our triumph."

Here I prove the validity of my work as a person of color who is proud of his "Euro-American" art roots and the aesthetic forms that those roots have generated and who also embraces a less obvious African art ancestry. (I use the term *Euro-American* for lack of a more substantial definition of the complex makeup/nature of this environment.) Here I also describe how this work translates and is relevant to a larger world order, mainly to that of the west coast of modern Africa. There are also obvious issues of gender and misogyny that will have to be explored, how they are represented in this particular African American and African culture.

IV The Eumenides/Divination
Orestes becomes king of Mycenae. Exoneration. Athena quiets the Furies— humanizing them, offering a more human life, "more power." "The torches of our triumph." But what woman here is more human and more powerful? Again, how does the female element fit into this work with its sole male cast?

Divination is the work ritual of *Geography*, its passage ceremony. Here I find a new place that pretends to take care of my art logic and that is politically acceptable to the larger societal idea of my race responsibility perhaps falsely. Again, "an ancestry of dark fate." Divination is not a return to Map but it is another kind of exile and a relevant one. In Divination the Africans experience something completely different from their tradition.

What of it is relevant and useful to their culturally different journeys?

A ROUGH-DRAFT PHYSICAL PERFORMANCE SCENARIO

(Or, how the above information might translate to an experimental performance perspective. There are no real text, music, installation notes here, but this should give a general idea of a beginning narrative line to pursue and/or to change.)

Map:
Words are heard, a description of some kind of landscape. A partial view of a landscape owing to bedspring curtain and light. Bodies, ritual moving, possibly through the space, possibly constructing something. There is a purpose to everything. Everything here is shrouded by the curtain and manipulation of light. An isolation of exile. At one point a duet spread wide left and right between Moussa and myself to drum/s and tones, drum/s taking over or tone taking over; all other movement in this section is chorus to this duet. Near the end of this section a portal is created within the bedspring curtain to obtain a bedspring floor surface to fall/jump on as the remaining curtain flies from bottom back and up into fly space, becoming a ceiling.

Crime:
The momentary resolve of Map is illuminated. The stage is surrounded with piles of bottles, bedsprings, ladders topped with standing men and tire seats and a slow-turning fan. The physical intensity from the end of Map continues. There are ritualized "war games," culture clashes, shown in forms of abstracted dances. A display/range of how one can eliminate another person/culture because of politics. Emotion is staged. There is a detachment to the "violence." All of this is described in and from a movement, sound, and choreography base. There is an obvious order and logic to this section, a predestinational form, of sorts.

Trial:
A suspension from Crime. Perhaps an actual physicalized trial scene. Moussa lies on the floor, singing, while I dance solo to his music. My dancing is influenced by his West African phrase. Or, it is a dialogue between Carlos and myself. Accusations are made about culture and choices. Autobiographical, confessional, storytelling, etc. (Again, differences are displayed through language, music, and movement.) An exposure to an examined confrontation of cultures, i.e., American, Western European, African. A kind of chaos. I think that the strongest connection would be between Moussa, representing Africa, and myself, with Carlos as an "African-American shadow," my interface.

Divination:

Bottle curtain rises. An exoneration, of sorts. A respite that moves toward a harmony that is relative and no obvious transcendence to any specific point. An unpredictable uncertainty, static; there is a tension but also a quiet that comes from gaps in conversation. This section could be described simply, with just voices and standing bodies, a battle of voices. Should the landscape also change?

Cast (an idea of roles, and again, not for the recognition of an audience):

Themselves/Orestes	Ralph (America)
Themselves/Clytemnestra/chorus	Carlos/Moussa (America/Guinea)
Themselves/Agamemnon/chorus	Moussa/Carlos (Guinea/America)
Themselves/Aegisthus/chorus	Djédjé (Côte d'Ivoire)
Themselves/Electra/chorus	Olivier (Côte d'Ivoire)
Themselves/Athena/chorus	Angelo (Côte d'Ivoire)
Themselves/Apollo/chorus	James (Côte d'Ivoire)
Themselves/Cassandra/chorus	Nai (Côte d'Ivoire)
Themselves/Plyades/chorus	Carlos (America)

Drummers/musicians: voices/chorus

Moussa (Guinea)
Goulei (Côte d'Ivoire)
Tapé (Côte d'Ivoire)

As I mentioned earlier, *Geography*, above all else, will be an exploration of foreign physical and language sensibilities, how they collide and intersect within my conceptual formal concerns.

Some specific physical, movement, choreography ideas:
- Creating a new physical language
- Exploring new physical rituals based on traditional African rituals and on postmodern dance forms
- Exploring the possibilities of improvisation in my work to an African music context
- Exploring a place for my fully fledged Euro-American moving within this foreign stage.
- Exploring the possibilities of African improvisation concerns (to silence and American abstract music sounds?)
- Exploring the influence of the European French classical "minuet" to

French-speaking traditional West African dancing.
- Exploring the physical descriptions of traditional African rhythms and gestures.
- Exploring the possibilities of the modern "urban" physical influences of Africa and America to African and American dancing.
- Exploring a physicalizing of dramatic elements/scenes from the *Oresteia*

(And, how do all of the above ideas relate to the installation, sound/music score and text?)

Other physical and theatrical-image ideas (referring to specific sections of the work's concept and installation): Dancing on different surfaces: concrete blocks, overturned boats, etc. Bodies in clay. Bodies in mud. An image of a literal blood-bath. Hosing bloodied bodies down. A firing squad, stylized murders. Young boys strapped to the torsos of men. The throwing of rocks. Silent and physically still bodies. And more to come.

Notes for the collaborators: The text, installation, and sound of this work should find a balance that is completely integrated into the weave of its fundamentally seamless movement and silence-based experience (the place where I begin)

Text notes/ideas from earlier discussions, plus: I see text in three sections of the work; Map, Trial, Divination. It is possible that there could be text in the Crime section but at this point that is not certain.

1. Some appropriate referencing/reinterpretation from the *Oresteia* narrative and from Ralph's own autobiographical notes.
2. Map/Agamemnon: monologue(with possible chorus), describing this "other" world. Words floating, exploding, disappearing, etc., through the space. Speaker is seen or not. Other bodies are on stage in a "ritualized" process arranging/rearranging this place. (Stringing bottles?)
3. Live interviewing of Africans, being asked questions or asking questions that Tracie asked originally "broken languages:"
4. Trial/*Eumenides*: An accusation duet/s and or an actual trial text
5. Divination: A chorus of many voices. All performers exposed on stage with standing mikes.
6. Africans and Americans telling their own stories.

Installation notes/ideas from earlier discussions, plus: This work should describe an "urban" otherworld, not one of "huts and villages."

I think that two basic looks will be a valiant adventure, plus objects to sit on that can be moved around. Enormity of scale will be very important (large or small). I will need forty by forty feet of empty physical stage space for the performance.

1. Bottle curtain idea is good but I'm not so sure that it could move throughout the performance. This needs to be discussed. The use of motors with sound will complicate the sound, music, text score (needs discussion)
2. Carts stacked, questionable—implies too much of American commerce?
3. Old boats
4. Train tracks, hanging vertically (a reference from the fire-escape work)
5. Trees hanging upside down in the audience sitting area? Safety issue.
6. Giant blackboards as stage legs that can be written on. Vertical length.
7. A partially exposed glass aviary for birds and/or a deer to be seen at some point.
8. A pile of small-screen televisions and/or old transitor radios (plus the possible static sounds that these things make)
9. Something built during the performance by the performers.

There are many lighting possibilities that could affect a look or looks of the installation. Two possible looks could be created with just light.

Sound Music notes/ideas:
The sound and music parts will have to be very controlled because of the many elements involved in the work and my penchant for plain silence.

Francisco's work will be less problematic to the flow of a physical narrative because his work is sparse, direct, and emotionally minimal. His work can easily describe an abstruse mood or landscape and it can be powerful. His work can also sound as "silence" and "incidental." I hear his score for parts of Map and Divination and there are probably more possibilities. But I will have to wait and see how the text is being constructed and how my physical ideas evolve before making any decisions about music placement, especially those decisions about simultaneous sound and text. I had originally thought that twenty to twenty-five minutes would be an appropriate amount of music for each composer but I think that we will need to wait until the first workshop before making any other concrete decisions. And then the final direction will have to be mine, based on what I think works best for the whole.

Paul Miller's work will be more challenging to place in the overall weave. I'm interested in what "more musical" and conceptual elements he can bring to the work. His work, music has the potential to be more demanding of focus and so whatever focus it brings has to be appropriate. His work also has the potential to give the African traditional sound an interesting perspective. I hear his score in parts of Crime, Trial, and perhaps, Divination. He will record with the musicians so that there will be something recorded that they can play with live, and it might be interesting to have him instruct one or more of the Africans to DJ live during the performances. All of these musical elements can fit into this work, playing off of other, seemingly contradictory elements. But it will all have to be controlled and that can't really happen until I start to hear some of the various "voices" of the collaborators.

As it stands, some physical work (my work with Carlos and Moussa in March and April), the text elements, and some installation ideas will be the first explored parts of the process, explored before the African process in June (Paul won't be recording until that time). I'm not sure if I will have any sound placement certainties before then but the preliminary information from Tracie, Nari, and myself should give what comes later a more obvious placement. I will continue to e-mail and discuss my rapidly forming ideas with everyone throughout this time.

As I mentioned earlier, in both of these scores there is the possibility of combining Tracie's text, or not.

When I woke up it was after two hours and there was no air. Next door someone was washing something in the sound of a sink, all night. I turned the air conditioner on and went back to wandering through my resolved thinking.

In the morning, my slave, of this circumstance, was waiting outside the door for my departure. He carried my bags down the narrow, dim hallway and knew less of my destination than I. Outside we found an empty car and drove, passing trees and graffitied walls, one proclaiming, "hyeanas were hermaphrodites." After four days we arrived at an airport. The slave gave me a *croix du roi* (cross of a king), which was exactly half of his most valuable possessions. He then kissed me and said that in a few years, when he was ready that he would come and help me again. He had no money to return home and I gave him what soft and sweating currency I had left over.

I also gave him two pages from my notes (so that he could practice his English):

> "My mind/eyes break down first, then my emotions. My body will take the longest because it is monogamous, stubborn. I am confronted with the startling difference between ideas and reality."

> "The Africans are very excited about coming to America and consider me an "ancestor"—a "big brother." But I don't trust translations and this consideration could mean anything."

> "I am in awesome gravity, standing among these men who seem like the most beautiful humans I have ever seen, and I am going crazy calculating how this beauty relates to what I know of my intent/work."

> "I danced in front of the village yesterday, on their concrete; it took two days to find the courage. They said that they could see the "African source" in my moving. They said that my dancing was similar to the dancing in the Cameroon. Today my back and knees hurt."

> "One of the drummers came up to me later and asked if he could stay with me, live where I lived when he comes to the U.S. and that he did not want to stay in a hotel. He thought that it would be better for the group to be in the same place, like their village, so that we could "talk" about things. Another suspicious translation."

> "Last night I had a severe attack of self doubt. I took some Rescue Remedy and closed my eyes. I woke up the next morning and felt as though there

were still some fight left in me, that I could fight against the desire to stop this journey and go back to something simple, American. It is a war, especially here. I feel stronger in the mornings."

"There is so much talent here. But I have to work to see it. Much of the surface of this talent has been informed by colonialism, even "spandex unitards," and the directness of the older tradition becomes a parody of what it is/was. Would apartheid, which strips a human of dignity but perhaps not an identity, have been better than the more subtle form of colonial slavery, which seduces an older identity into another form, one that tries to please, forever after awkward? An incredibly stupid American question."

"Already this is the hardest thing that I have ever done."

I watched the slave walk away, knowing that he would continue to walk for weeks back to his home. I wondered what he needed the money for.

I am lying at the bottom of the ocean. In these seconds I have no body, only the personality of my heart, only the neurosis of my heartbeat. Other bodies swim by and eat bits of me. I watch with horror the pieces collapsing, waterlogged. What happened to the blood? Every time I am touched I take on another layer of filth, ancient bacteria, hatred. I am obsessed with washing my body. Even now I am taking a vast shower, holding my breath and almost passsing out. The next time I will use a wide transparent yellowed tape to cover my lips. Sooner or later I will learn to breathe through opacity. But to do this successfully I will have to bow my face downward. What I will see is something that occassionally pokes out from my lower abdomen. It raises its head when I am not thinking, poking its head upward into the wall of muscle and skin like the head of a snake. When I try to touch it, it returns down and disappears.

There is a light coming from somewhere. It has the haze of one single fluorescent bulb. It is either that or it is dark. Someone is nearby. It stays dark. There is a smell, not a stink, but stale perfumed flesh, all dressed up, erect, planned.
His shirt is white with huge polka dots of blue, yellow, red and, of course, wet. There are also four large leaves, also blue. He is sitting and playing a guitar. The guitar is held together with Scotch tape, waterproof, really, but the sound is sweet anyway. Later the sound haunts me to death because it is not rhythmic. It is my homework—how it is relevant.

Fan in room 203
Hotel Bergnido
Abidjan

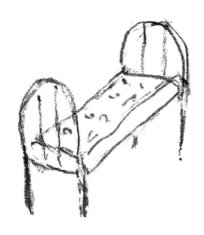

My bed in room 203
Hotel Bergnido
Abidjan

58

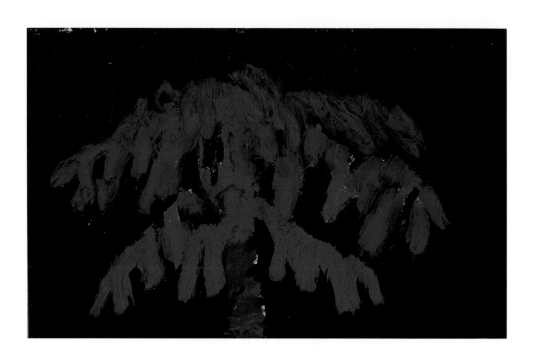

Mostly cement and no porch

The beautiful sewing machines in the central market

AFRICAN violet

When I was puking in
this sink I was in the same
position that i pray In

The look of a Glass of water in Kumasi-because there was no electricity.

A BICHÉ

a deer
goat?

a biché looks like a small deer

APRIL 1997

NEW YORK

Day 1

Moussa came in with drum but no dance clothes. He wore a white T-shirt backward over a beige African protection tunic and French jeans with a Senegalese beaded belt that reminded me of the beadwork of South African artists. He is missing his first or second molar on the right or left side of his mouth. His hair is short and groomed in small, naturally manicured bushes. His irises are the same glowing brown of the scleras and pupils. His skin is the color born of dun and purple. At one point we take our shirts off and the structure below his skin seems perfect, I have more mass. He shows me his feet, the scars, calluses, and broken bones. They match his hands in how the flesh below the nails is tinted ochre. His wife says that he looks like me. I don't know how that is possible. Moussa moves like a deer.

I demonstrated an arbitrary series of movements, the way in which I happened to be moving that day. He imitated the first movement and seamlessly transformed it into one of the things that he masters, teaching traditional Guinean steps. I followed along. Occasionally he would smile but it became clear that this expression was cast not out of happiness but only to demonstrate a freedom in the movement of the head. At the end of three hours he began to see me "let go"—I would say, begin to expire.

Moussa is a Malinke griot, from a family of griots. When he was a baby he was placed underneath a balafon to sleep with his father's rhythms. Rhythm is everything to him. I must use it. There is no collaboration without it. That is shocking. I am reminded, with some amusement, of Nancy Hauser and 1976 and Bach.

He is demanding a responsibility from me that I mold into drama.
I have prepared for this week and had no idea that it would be beyond preparation.

There is another powerful agenda at play, nameless. It got let loose yesterday after rehearsal and I could not sleep. Volatile, useful, if I can calm myself.

Notes:
1. Try to communicate more of my expectations.
2. Can he be directed?

Day 2

Communicating is hard. My French is not enough and his English cannot decipher vague ideas. Moussa is able to communicate that he wants to work every day. Today we continued with his movement, which I am immediately not interested in dancing but in which I am allowing myself to fall apart. I almost passed out at one point because of this challenge of dismissal. I took a break and went to the men's room to be alone, to splash water on my face. When I returned, Moussa was lying on the floor, legs crossed and arms behind his head, singing a song that he had written in his original language.

Exquisite and unchoreographable.

At the end of the day I find the courage to demonstrate another formally random something from my body, something that I thought would translate, something crooked. I am not sure how it worked, I looked but couldn't really see his body adapting. It was. There were moments in these two days of possible pay dirt, if I can find a dignity and an elegance. My muscles and bones feel challenged.

Notes:
I'm not sure how much I can push him.

Day 3

I took an extraordinary amount of difficult time walking to rehearsal today. I was late and Moussa was early. I walked in and he was looking out the window. I think that he knows that I am falling apart at this.

He played drums and I warmed up. I have yet to see him physically prepare for any of his dancing. He played many rhythms. I taped some of them and then we both danced, improvising to the recording. At this point, I had my first moment of inspiration that this collaboration could work.

At the end of the day I took him and his family out to dinner, a small repayment for a week of hereafter. Moussa wanted rice, which the restaurant did not serve.

Notes:
Moussa thinks that we can find a newer dance language. He wants this new information. He also wants help in getting an American visa for his older brother, who lives in Guinea.

NEW HAVEN: WE ARE ALL TOGETHER AND NOW INTO THE *ORESTEIA*

Moussa becomes Agamemnon, because he has two daughters and because the others feel that he is losing his Africa. Still, he is "kolo," the older brother.

Apollo is from the north and worships space. Before he started dancing he was homeless for five years. Apollo is the blackest, a dull black, like dark dirt. His features are flatter, less brilliant, than the others. He has thin trails of night water gliding down the back of his head. A cowry shell rests at the bottom of his forehead. The rest of his physique continues downward, skeletal-lean. He has no hips and no buttocks, just like Agamemnon. His legs are enormously long. There is no distinction between his moving up, down, and side. He is the most fragile, with fever, and weak knees and ripped feet and a need to marry someone American. He is mostly alone. He says that he was born weak and that that is why his arms are always crossed.

Athena is of the famous Baoule. His face is octagonal. New bones at the bottom of his jaw that are extremely decorative. His hair is pointed, short, crowned. He is shiny dark, glowing, as though his skin is about to grow something. Small miniature ears like the others, lobes extinct or eaten off at birth. He stands muscled, mythic and tight. On day 3 he bought a cellular phone and needed help with dialing a number that someone else had written on a piece of blue paper. It will be useless in Abidjan. It might be useless here. He also bought a pair of motorcycle boots. So did Apollo. Apollo has blisters on his heels from his new boots. Athena does not and he does not wear socks.

There are two Furies. One wears a helmet of hair, shadowed with slight parallel rows slanting down to his ears. He has grown taller and wider since August, an unusual bulk for a Fury. He is always moving, arms talking, singing, bouncing. His face and eyes are difficult to describe. The palms of his hands are a dark orange and they are as hard as tire rubber.

The other Fury has four thin locks of hair, each five inches long, jutting out from the top of his forehead. One of them is wrapped in an ancient thread. The rest of his head is shaved. He is the smallest Fury. He is as committed as the other furies but lets the others be more furious. His black is jet, keen. He wears shirts that are always falling to his knees, in the pocket a pack of expensive cigarettes. I have only seen him in one pair of jeans, culottes that creep out from below the long shirts and that have a rip in the left shin-length leg. He bought a pair of plastic sandals, pale blue, from K-Mart, a perfect match for his glistening feet and shins. And then one day he wore a pair of black, pleated, creased, long pants. No one took him serious that day.

Electra has minstrel eyes and Medusa hair, like small tressled tree trunks. Classically handsome. A narrow black giant whose feet spread like Cimmerian water lilies. His face and hair together are inside of black, an altogether brilliant dusk. His voice bellows out small songs and molded French in a very deep baritone. From lips that blossom out like a welcoming immense round bed.
"I am Electra-amber, daughter of Agamemnon. I wear the weave that I gave Orestes at birth, why I have bought no new dresses. Later I wrote him many, many letters."

Aegisthus, the other chief: Has a round pretty face, copper brown, shiny brown-red, Asiatic eyes, also brown; even his hair is brown but dark. A young griot in another language. He is small, slight, also round, a belly. A voice of nonadjusting density, sweet. He has not bought new shoes or T-shirts or caps but because of the food here he is growing fatter.

Pylades, my homeboy: Aegisthus said to me that when Pylades speaks English he has a hard time understanding him. Pylades' father is Puerto Rican. He has the brown-yellow color of race confusion. Sleepy eyes. A lion's mane of locks, glamorous. Flat-footed. Soft-muscled. A bad knee. One day Pylades was wrestling with Athena. Pylades was growling, aggressive. Athena remained sturdy and did not make a sound.

No one moves like Clytemnestra. They all don her dresses and walk with small strides of pelvis. But as men they are all avowed sexists. And love mother as flesh, one who nourishes lushly.

ON ORESTES

For a brief time Orestes is an actor. Orestes is also spring, like Eurydice, like Kore. Orestes and Electra are twins, radiant and lovers. For example: Because she murdered their father, Clytemnestra shows her tit to Orestes to save her life while Electra looks on feeling no compassion for the mother that raised her. She never knew her sacrificed sister to love. Neither did Orestes. "I have hated my mother often." "When my mother hated me I could not believe it and thought that she was some winged harpy."

"Chorus: Their bloody strife."

Clytemnestra had lost Iphigenia from her other tit before she was Iphigenia, the rest of her blood is dispensable and that is that.

This evening there is a theater event and there are two judges, both of them women. One of them decides that Orestes is not articulate enough in his speech and so excludes him from the performance. He had worked very hard and created something new for this particular event. His inherent tones are very emotional, evocative, but they are hard to understand. "Please speak Parnassian," they have often said. Electra has the articulation but she does not act.
There are three other performers in this evening of performances. They are all present and sit in armchairs, facing the judges when the announcement is made. One of them, whose name is Pylades, cares greatly for Orestes and bows his head at the news. Orestes has nothing to say, but someone does say "Destiny had a hand in that, my child."

In the building there are bleachers. Behind the bleachers stands a giant cinderblock wall. A procession forms. Most of the audience sits on the top row of the bleachers to rest their backs against the wall. There are very few people in attendance, most of them elderly, none of them judges. A photographer is present. He has loose black-and-white photographs of all the actors. He does not know now what to do with the ones of Orestes. None of them are for sale.

The performers are backstage rearranging, trying to decide a new order. Orestes is also there, constructing a forgetting. Pylades, the one who cares, considers Orestes a "goatkiller," one who can accomplish difficult tasks. He approaches Orestes and in a language they share encourages him, "Eh töörö." Orestes returns the sympathy, "And you give them hell, Pylades." He

continues his work, not completely accepting his friend's urn of compassion.
A few minutes pass and with a finality to his placement Orestes moves
beyond the others and walks through a door.

Then Orestes walks on stage and is seen anyway. His body has no angles
and his costume is a red suit. "I must escape this blood; it is my own." And
that is all that he says. The rest is a dance. It was not what he had planned.
It lasts only a moment and Orestes walks offstage. Afterwards no one has
comment. Only Electra is ecstatic and cannot believe how much of his body
is her own. It was hard for her to sit still. She too moved as he moved and
endured his breathing. Now Orestes sits in a dressing room and remembers
what else it was that he had wanted to say.
There is a knock on the door and it is Dionysus. He had not seen the small
act and thinks that he is somewhere else. He recognizes Orestes and wants
to take him into the hills to feast, to Le Sacrifice, a place where they can eat
tête de mouton *and drink rhum coke and beer. Orestes accepts, sensing, "He*
saved me." All the evening Dionysus appeals to Orestes that he is noble and
that he is not a racist, only that he hates all of mankind. Dionysus is very
drunk and smokes cigarettes like he drinks, inhaling even the flies down his
wide black throat. At one point he stops breathing but only a pause and this
is embarrassing because he has so much yet to say and in many, many
languages. When he is able to continue Dionysus then tells Orestes of
beautiful distant lands where some indigenous people are treated the same
as natives and foreigners and he tells him of the few people that he has
loved. Orestes sits across from him, finding a distance from the cloud that
surrounds Dionysus's ferine eyes and blazing teeth. Not once does Dionysus
insult Orestes.

It is late and there is no more food or drink. They wander out into a small
alley, legs oblivious to the ambivalent bush rats and to any productive
stepping. Dionysus wants to show Orestes more of the night. He wants to
drive Orestes to a place where there is dark water, torches, "something to
write about." He is crying. Orestes has had enough and wants to go to bed,
to a bed in Dionysus's palace (Electra is also lonely). Dionysus pleads and
falls to his knees for Orestes' company. Dionysus then pulls a pink, folded
piece of paper from his pocket and hands it to Orestes. On the paper is a
casual drawing of an antiquated automatic military weapon. To the right of
the drawing, in an exact pen, are written the words "I did not draw this. A
young man who works in the papeterie *across from the military base gave it*
to me." Orestes asks if he can keep the drawing. Dionysus nods and opens
the door to his palace. Orestes thanks him and moves inside. After a long

Orestes that he prefers the original because it is longer and that it gives him time to not take it seriously. He says, "I do not know what it is that you are saying, or why, but your sounds are unique and they make me feel unprotected and since I am a god and unafraid of you that is OK. Your movement was more familiar, satisfying, a guiltless language of bones and spirit. It reminded me of the movement of a people in the north that I have seen who no longer exist." Orestes replies, "Yes, all of my motives are based on loss." Apollo then tells Orestes that if he had been a judge that he would have let him go on. He also tells Orestes that he thinks a younger audience would help. Orestes does not know where to place that last information.

There is a moment during the day when the clouds conceal the sun. Their shelter gives the appearance of shrouded early morning light, repeating itself.

Electra is waiting when Orestes leaves the temple. As they walk down the precise dirt roadway from Delphi, Electra asks Orestes what will happen now, now that he no longer belongs to the theater. Orestes has no answer. Electra tells Orestes that she would like to go to their father's gravesite. Orestes has no other plans.

They signal a car service. They stop off at their house first. They change their clothes to black and later arrive at the site of their father. They have no flowers. They stand together at the mounded grave neither moving nor speaking. There is no kneeling. No one prays. There is no embracing. There is no whispering. There are no sudden warnings and therefore no sudden turning around. They do not imagine where is the grave of Clytemnestra, their mother. And because Iphigenia was a small baby girl her bones must be blown somewhere far away in the mountains, at the foot of some tree. There is no blood. There are no Furies here. There is no ghost. Certainly no Ogun. There is no wind blowing and therefore no sound from the grass. There are no footsteps. There is no brilliant sky but it is still day and so their figures, shapes, are not obscured, no direct light intercepted by inpenetrable objects projecting a refuge. There are no shadows.

Puerto Angel, Oaxaca
February 1997

WORKSHOP I

Performers

from Guinea/U.S.	Djeli Moussa Diabaté
from Groupe Ki-Yi M'bock Côte d'Ivoire	Djédjé Djédjé
	Nai Zou
	Goulei Tchépoho
	Zaoli Mabo Tapé
from Ensemble Koteba Côte D'Ivoire	Akpa Yves Didier, "James"
	Kouakou Yao, "Angelo"
from U.S.	Carlos Funn
	Ralph Lemon

Text	Tracie Morris
Visual Art	Nari Ward
Soundscores	Francisco López
	Paul D. Miller (DJ Spooky, That Subliminal Kid)
Sensors	Paul D. Miller, (DJ Spooky, That Subliminal Kid) realized with Ralph Lemon
Costume Design	Liz Prince
Lighting Design	Stan Pressner
Sound Design	Rob Gorton
Production Dramaturgy	Peter Novak and Katherine Profeta
Stage Management	Jenny Friend
English/French Interpretation	Orida Boukhezer-Diabaté
Company Manager	Carla Jackson
Assistant Director	Weir Harman
Videographers	Weir Harman and Bill Mack

May 12

Met with Paul M. He wants to sound-sense the performers using Radio Shack motion detectors, composition as object. This could work perfectly in relationship to Francisco's chaste participation. Definitely more work for me. Met with Tracie. Her text is moving toward what I aesthetically imagine. That I can already imagine it is probably not a good thing in the long run, but for now I'm happy. Liz Prince will do costumes. Everything is now in place.

May 21

There are visa problems. I canceled French today, my last class. Overextended. I cannot imagine canceling a single rehearsal at Yale but nothing to do with this project is proving to be conventional, especially my discipline.

The Africans arrive in four days and my insides stay bereft. I hope that I feel better soon. I'm excited and exhausted. I can't imagine sustaining this body type for four weeks.

May 22

It occurs to me that I'm exaggerating how hard this project will be. Everyone else seems quite simple about what they think it is. Diane Madden (from Trisha Brown Co.) told me that it sounds like a great project, "for everyone else."

May 28

New Haven: The Africans have arrived with much dazzling energy. We began by improvising, introducing ourselves with our distinct cultural rhythms. The language differences, the bodies, the interpretations of art are all astonishingly out of sync. The Africans are happy and I cannot imagine creating anything in this environment. I'm swimming, feeling emotions I have never felt before. I don't know what it is that I'm doing. None of my acknowledged skills seem important here. My instincts tell me that I must give in to my body. I don't have a bathtub. We will do yoga at the beginning of each day.

May 29

Day 3 feels like day 100. A giant collapsing into one threatening world deeper into another. Yesterday I taught some movement from a phrase that I have been working on. They all jumped on it like fresh food to an almost starving body. In the beginning it was very exciting, and then it was clear that most of them move like all bodies that do not embrace the straight and vertical logic of European/American dance training. A muscular and directional struggle, among other things. There are moments when I want to give in to the division of our worlds, leave them side by side and honest. But I think that it will be more heroic to stick with what at the moment seems impossible. Disintegration? I have many sound and image certainties that pop up often. The ease of these ideas is somewhat disturbing in context of the larger challenges of what I want and need from the Africans and what the Africans are prepared to give. I'm consumed.

May 30
Moussa and Tapé got into a discussion about drumming. Côte d'Ivorian and Guinean. Moussa is an elder and Tapé's tradition is to respect his elders. But he does not have much interest in Moussa's rhythms. Moussa thinks that they can work out their problem but Tapé seems to want to acquiesce, which is not working out the problem. It began with me. I taped a rhythm from Moussa's drumming in March and then gave it to Tapé to compose something innovative from Moussa's original rhythmic idea. I did not think to ask Moussa if this was an acceptable transgression. Now I know.

May 31
The music discussion continued into the evening over beer and basketball and I heard that some things were worked out. I'm curious.

We practiced more contact improvisation work yesterday and they were aggressive with it and raw. There are possibilities.

We worked on new phrases, one from Djédjé and one from my work. Both phrases have a base in rhythmic steps and this seems to be a solution for realistic choreographic translations. A good day.

Nari is here and his input is direct and spacious. He spoke of creating images that are expected and how it's important to challenge those images, to see what other tension might be found.

I had the men wear suits at one point in the day and it was wonderful and disconcerting. American cool, African, Eurocentric, what? I'm headed in all the right directions. Still, my work is enormous.

the drum is basic,
complicated. the heart.
but common, somewhat
monotonous and redundant
it is one voice that
is always percussive.
a problem of tonal
and textural variation.
and the drum is
a giant of "tradition"
representation.

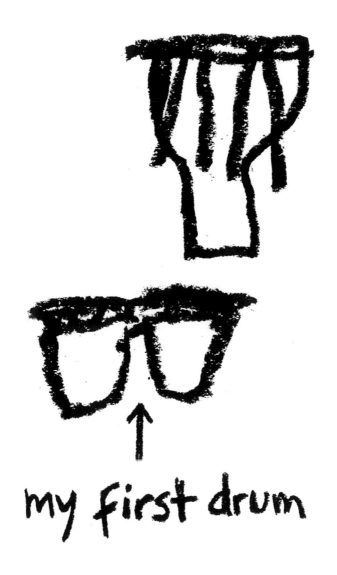

my first drum

I will separate the drums
and let them represent
a purity, unadorned, and
powerful. But it will
be important to try to find
an appropriate structure
so that the drums have a
frame to command that
basic reference.

Bongos

DJEMBE

June 1

Another forward progress day. For the first time I feel, on momentary indescribable levels, the confidence that this process could work. At least it is a good fiery beginning. I thought that I would end rehearsal early, I felt emotionally exhausted but by dinner break there was an unpredictable surge of momentum. There are moments when I experience that most of the work here is already done, or simply waiting to explode. At the moment I'm not a choreographer, only a catalyst. And this is not art but ethno-anthropology. But not really.

June 3

And back two steps. Yesterday disappeared without fanfare. At the end of the day I fell back into a mire of uncertainty. But I'm on schedule. The movement part of this work will be and is what is life-altering, therefore my familiar emotions in this realm have no chance of survival. One plan is to daily expire. Another interesting reality here is that I don't have anyone around who could support my groomed aesthetic, to challenge my more immediate responses and to give this experience a historical perspective. The roller coaster.
James could be a modern dancer. Moussa has the hardest tasks dancing outside of his form.
The whole group sings a different praise to our daily yoga beginning.

June 4

Ann, Jenny T., Baraka Sele, and Linda Walton came up to New Haven yesterday to meet with the Yale crew, and to watch. Helpful. I continued working on phrases; some moments continue to interest me but most lose a specialness quickly. I named the phrases, giving them names that chart the journey from "art" to whatever and whereever it is we are going. I did not eat yesterday and then my mind stopped working. Nari remains excited.

June 5

Yesterday we continued work on the Collage Phrase, a mélange of steps from the various foreign traditions of the group, plus a few physical disruptions from my passive-aggressive physique. Their footwork and rhythm astounds. The phrase has great possibilities but scares me because it is so brilliant, dazzling and immediately entertaining. We also worked on a more physical theatrical idea where one man throws another onto the floor and then they softly help each other back up to start again. Pina Bausch goes to Africa and then Harlem. Sketches, sketches.

dans ce

dans ce paradis

dans ce paradis

comme

l'enfer

nous affirmons un Dieu

inversé

Ceci est soit un vide

soit une lumière aveuglante

de

en toute façon je ne vois rien

que bleu

NÊ NÉ

[2X]

NE NÉ LA GO

NA GOLÔ NÉ DE

ÊLÊHÊ ,

ÊWLOLÉ

GLOU NAKOSS

OU M

A OUINI LE LA GO BOLO
YA ZIG bALE

ÊNI ÊLÊHÊ FÊTÊ
YO U) A NI GI GUÊ

ÊLÊHÊ ZÊRÉ

Ê YOBÔ NÉ NI YO bO
ÊNI BE YIRI GUÊ

93

At the end of the day I had them translate some of Tracie's text into their original languages, for a text exercise, experiment. James became upset because I had suggested something that seemed to him a school exercise. He made it very clear to me that he had quit school to dance and did not see the point of this exercise.

June 6

The dancers are starting to fall. New pains, damaged feet, and exhaustion. I will now need to be more careful as I plow ahead. My anatomy seems impenetrable. We continue to work in scraps of movements and ideas. There does not seem to be any other choice as I search for what I don't understand.

June 8

Fighting a cold, fighting the cold temperature. Moussa's neck is out, Nai is recovering from a sore lower back, and Carlos is still battling the flu. Yesterday we worked early. I added some hand gestures to Djédjé's Pygmy Dance, a Central African bush dance he interpreted from an Abidjan television program. I'm happy with a few of the gestures but doubt that even the few will survive.
After the morning rehearsal we went to a neighborhood party and ate fried and barbecued chicken and potato salad. The Africans played drums and danced and everyone was happy. They did not seem to mind that they were on exhibition; in fact they seemed to love it.
We were scheduled to rehearse after the party but I found it impossible to pull my energy back into a creative focus so I let everyone go home. A disappointment.

June 10

I felt like a complete failure from beginning to the end of yesterday. Nothing seemed to work. Perhaps due to an inadvertent step onto a landmine. I instigated a discussion of trance dancing, my interest in the physicality of it. I suggested an improvisation. An attempt at letting go of the common thought processes that follow a moving physical form. I tried to demonstrate by showing *Divine Horsemen*, the Maya Deren movie, mostly about Haitian Voudoun in the 1940s, which Djédjé called "fake," because of the posthumous editing and soundtrack. In the film, most of the movement of possession has been slowed down. "I witness a remarkable physical abandon, freedom." Tracie, sitting quietly throughout my presentation, jumped to her feet, "There is no freedom in the trance physicality—It's not a liberation from the body that you see on the video. They're being mounted by the God. It isn't abandon, even though it may look like it—rather his body is transformed by the God. There's no liberty of movement there." The dancers all agree. I agreed, already knowing this to be true. Desperately trying to find a better language I constructed a not too thought out exercise, where we broke into partners, one supporting the other so that the supported persons could improvise abandon, without falling and hurting themselves. I partnered Nai, who almost fell into a real trance, a detail I discovered later. Nai had recently been in a trance while in Africa and it took his spiritual guide four hours to get him out of it. It was clear that all the performers knew and had experienced trance and thought the idea too dangerous for this environment, especially Djédjé, "We can simulate it if you want, but it'll look ridiculous." James wanted to experiment with my vague request but conditioned it by saying that if he went far enough, which could happen, that nothing in the theater could control it. "What you would need to stop me, you don't have here." Moussa said that each of the Africans has a different relationship to trance. He seems less awed with the supernatural and yet it is a real part of his life. He wants to continue exploring the idea, which seems to have hit a brick wall. At the end of the night we worked on Tracie's text, which was a respite. God, dance is an impossible form.

June 11
A little better day. Plowing ahead in inches. The onlookers, those not dancing are sensing a stall, after all, it is week 3. Little do they know that things slow down rather than speed up. It's all to do with the energy and the thickness of buried mass. My eyes often return to seeing what I remember. So progress feels even more impossible. I keep trying.

June 12
Most of the day was spent trying to show the Africans how to contact the floor without hurting themselves. They are all sore. My body is feeling remarkably well. Francisco arrived with a collection of recorded material. He sat us all down in the theater, turned off all the lights and created a sightless performance of colossal sound. At first I thought that what I was hearing would be too powerful for this work. He assured me that anything is possible with what he has brought along. Showed a few seconds of some of the work that is in better shape than not to Francisco, Stan P., Nari, and other production collaborators, and it seems hopeful. Stan W drops in on rehearsals often. Sits in the back of the theater. Often we go out to lunch. We never talk about what he sees. I wonder what kind of angel he is. The Bulls won last night and Jordan helps me get through another day. The Africans seem to prefer Pippen.

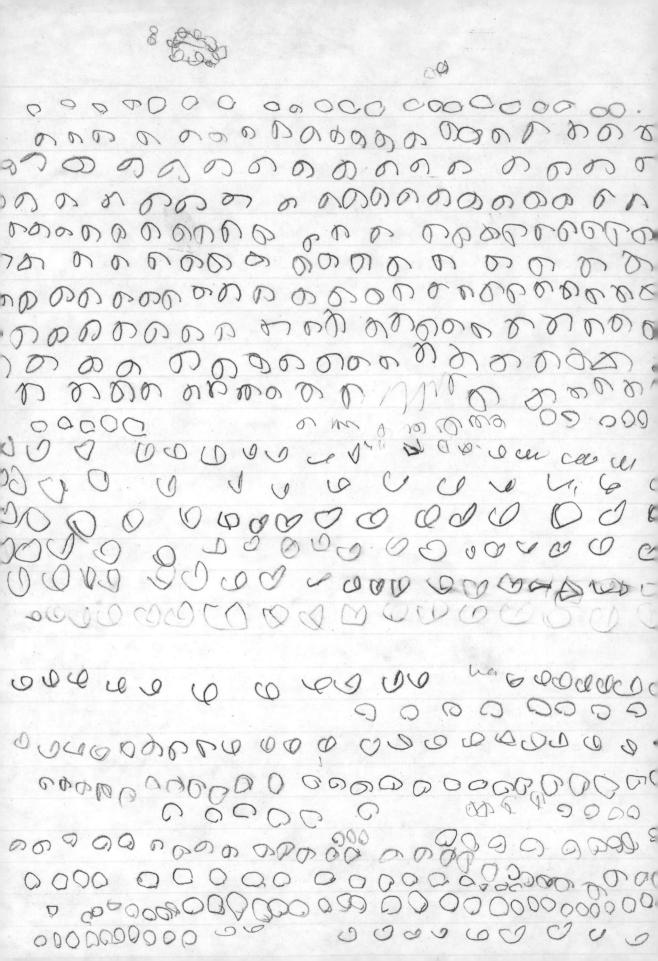

June 13

Barometric pressure or something like that, that's what I feel like this morning. We inch along. Progress is made very slowly and I think that this could be a problem. I'm also very bothered by the cloth weaving in the set/installation's bedsprings, too graphic, something like that. I would like to watch the unadorned, and obvious, many connected bedsprings. An image that Nari finds too untextured. Other than this soft impasse the collaboration with Nari has been without flaw. All the other collaborative elements are in my aural and visual comprehension, control, at the moment. I think that the Africans feel very important here, dignified. We improvised yesterday, "avec batterie," and everyone danced their personal tradition, a freedom I have not allowed for two weeks. It completely cleansed the space. The rest of the day was a muscular magic.

June 14

Yesterday was Friday the thirteenth and it was a good day. Put together the contact Bach Dance and it looks as if it will work. We also worked on a variation of the failed trance idea with James, Moussa, and Carlos. What I'm after is a stage event not an actual possession. Trance is not the point. "I went home and thought about the trance dancing issue some more. I think it's something that you as artists cannot separate from your lives. Maybe for you there is nothing else between being in trance and faking it. But Carlos and I have been talking about a certain kind of freedom we can access. Because Carlos and I are Americans and we don't relate to the visual form of that movement in the same way, it's easier for us to access that otherworldly movement without it being imitative or going into a trance. I saw the videotape and I wanted to exploit it, because it is visually engaging. But I don't understand it physically or spiritually. So, I would like to turn things around." I would call what I set up an improvisation but something beyond that was in progress. I played a Francisco composition of a tone that goes from extreme quiet to extreme volume in the course of twenty minutes. James and Moussa had their eyes closed the whole time, moving slowly, without recognizable rhythms and "steps," and somehow kept from falling off the stage. Carlos found it almost impossible to move, lying in a ball in the middle of the space. He wants house music, a "pulse," and the club, an easier access for him. Moussa was exhausted. I had asked them all to find some internal reason to move unbounded. We all eventually arrived at sleep.

James is interested in continuing my research but says that he needs to go back to Abidjan to get protection from someone, something there so that nothing bad happens.

June 16

I went to New York last night and saw some French modern dance. Barely able to sit in my seat. Nothing made movement sense or very little of it had relevance to my work here with the Africans. I couldn't wait to get back on the train.

June 17

A raucous day. We started with some simple singing ideas that I had and that the Africans snatched away and made into another more interesting musical experience. I had a breakthrough with Moussa, finally. He plays his jun jun, sets it gently on the floor, and then dances a solo in silence and then repeats the action. It is one of the strongest images that I have seen thus far. The drum stripped from the dance. I also made a solo on Angelo that he digested, sort of, and that I then translated back into my body. Quite different from what it was.

June 18

Production meeting with all the collaborators. Our first informal showing of sketches and ideas. Most of it works and it can all work better, especially my parts, which I have no time to rehearse. Not much of a narrative at the moment. It felt good to perform. Now what? The work has a definite look to it, raw.
Tapé's back went into spasm on Monday and he was in bed all of Tuesday.
Goulei filled in remarkably well.

June 19

Once a week I seem to hit these pockets where I begin to shut down, even in the midst of revelations. But I've been told that I have protection from the Africans and their boundlessness. It is inspiring to me that I'm not ready to go as far as they are capable of going. Carlos might be physically falling apart. His breakfast of Pop-tarts is not encouraging.

June 24

The end of workshop I. I have a complete picture of all the parts and can now go away and digest where to begin. Mostly I go away with a profound sense of being interested in the humanness of the Africans, and how that seems to affect everyone else involved. A great demand for respect here. I do not feel the panic I felt before I entered this new environment. This work is only half art and there are moments when that comforts me. The Africans will go away and find new info to bring back, something that they have always done. Carlos leaves tonight for Richmond, Virginia, to partake in a modern dance concert. I have a lot of work to do.

June 25

A fête. A good-bye dancing party with pizza and a keg of beer, which the Africans found fascinating. A nice finish. I'm very tired. African music, American music—in both there are some things missing. African dancing, American dancing—in both there are some things missing.

REPOSE

AUGUST 10–19: MAINE

water shore rocks erosion grass and small trees porch shack one room
chair me

water shore rocks erosion grass and small trees porch shack one room chair
Later I will practice following the slope of the ground.

a shore grass that measures three and a half feet to the top of its two-inch cluster
blows left left left and then it is still.

a perfect boat. harbored at the end of the bay. crafted wooden skeletal skiff outline.
no one floats it. becoming water and pier.

there is a small island with forty-three trees in the harbor that you can walk to if the
tide is low enough. but you have to be careful because the water can return very
quickly without apparent warning and leave you stranded in a moated empty forest.

How to build a wall from stones discarded from the sea:
1. Choose flat rocks whenever possible
2. Exact symmetry should be avoided
3. Try not to predict its life span

Enough of faultless rocks. A contrary variant: Compiling specific planks from ancient
lobster traps. Each dating from a different season and decay. Using their original
crooked nails whenever possible. I built a ladder out of dried driftwood. It stands
exactly twenty-two inches high.

I went to sit in a cabin on an ocean. There was a small boy there who was without a
father. And we became friends. My desire to be without caved into his cunning child
earth. My isolation forfeited, I meditated on his knowledge of knots and tides.

WORKSHOP II

August 21

The Africans return in a day or two. With great anticipation my body screams to be alone. Desert, ocean, tree, whatever. I do love it. I have a teacher, a Shingon monk. A very alert human being who once said to me that he doesn't like being around people very much. His is spiritual support. I suppose some of us have a hard time processing more than one face, voice, body at a time. And then there are the distractions of sky hues, moon periods, and wind.

I saw a photo of Nari's original bottle curtain in the Sunday *New York Times* while visiting the Shaker community in Maine. (Bottles dug up from a celibate community's graveyard.) And wondered what relationship the Shakers have with the Africans.

August 23

Orida called at 7:00 A.M. this morning to tell me that Abidjan had called and the Africans were lost. Not on their scheduled Sabena flight. And could land at either JFK or Newark on American, TAP, TWA, Delta, at any time during the day or night. Carla found them on TWA and they did end up at JFK at 1:09, six minutes earlier than their original expected time. Half of their drum supply was left in Lisbon. They all seemed very tired.

I feel like I'm starting over. Too much time in my cabin on the ocean, in Maine, (where I saw one black face, walking into the L. L. Bean outlet in Ellsworth).

I'd rather be playing baseball.

Tomorrow we drive up to Pam and Judd Weisberg's Art Awareness in Lexington, New York for a two-week residency. The bush.

August 24

A morning of regret. Missing my cat and the quietness of my house. Picked up the van and drove through the empty Sunday streets of New York. Picked up the Africans and Tracie Morris.

The drive to Lexington was a party with music from Côte d'Ivoire blaring the whole way. Nai dressed up in a blue double-breasted blazer for the trip.

Lexington is rustic and the Africans are happy that we are only here for two weeks. I'm on the other side of something. Less intimidated this time inside.

August 25

James walked into the main house this morning shaking uncontrollably. They all apparently slept well last night, warm enough in their mountain cabins. But from under the blankets, to the cold mountain air and floor was a challenge. Part of the shopping list today is thermal underwear. They had no concept of this mildly cold

August climate. We are all up by eight, so work can start earlier than previously planned.

James, Angelo, Nai, Moussa have a new relationship to Walkmans that did not exist during the last workshop. It's interesting watching them listen, move and sing to barely audible rhythms.

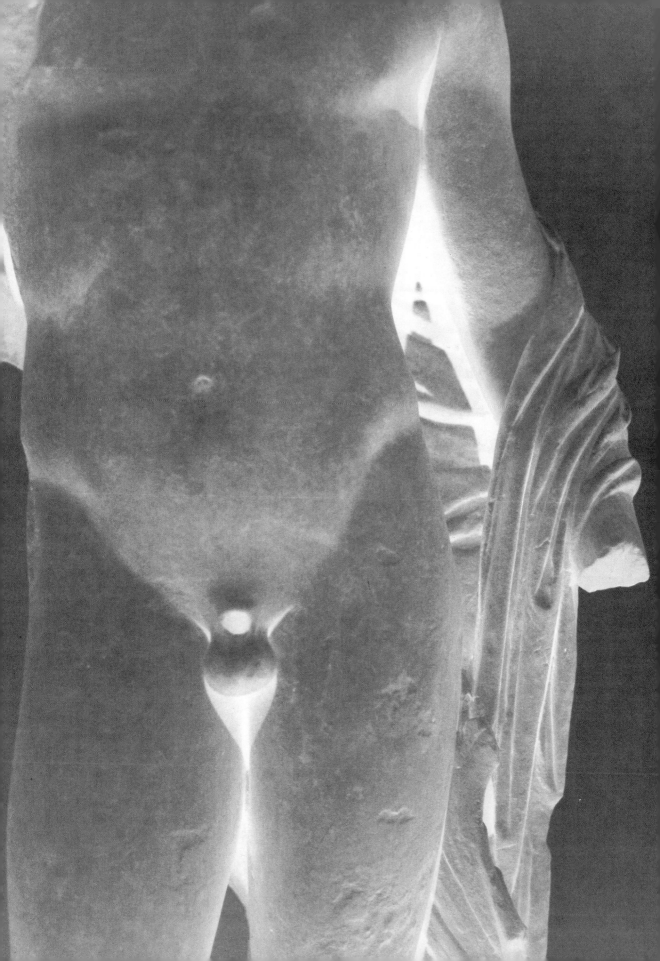

YOUNG APOLLO

"The worst sores of all are the tropical eating sores (ulcus phagedenicum tropicum), *which spread in all directions. Not infrequently a whole leg surface is one single sore, in which the sinews and bones show like white islands. The pain is frightful, and the smell is such that no one can stay near the patient for any length of time. The sufferers are placed in a hut by themselves, and have their food brought to them; there they gradually waste away and die after terrible sufferings. This most horrible of all the different sores is very common on the Ogowe, and merely to disinfect and bandage does no good. The sufferer must be put under an anesthetic and the sore carefully scraped right down to the sound tissue, during which operation blood flows in streams. The sore is then bathed with a solution of permanganate of potash, but a careful inspection must be made every day so as to detect any new purulent center that may show itself, as this must at once be scraped out like the others. It is weeks, perhaps months, before the sore is healed, and it will use up half a case of bandages. What a sum it costs us, too, to feed the patient for so long! But what joy when—limping, indeed, for the healed wound leaves the foot permanently deformed, but rejoicing at his freedom from the pain and stench—he steps into the canoe for the journey home!*
Albert Schweitzer, 1914, Congo*

He promised the doctor that he was finished with women. He is on antibiotics and sleeps most of the day. In the van, on the way to a laundromat, he slept through the radio news of Princess Diana's death. Perhaps his urine has burned for a long time. He is lucky because he is not yet blind. He made me promise not to tell any of the women in our group. But they all knew something was wrong days before I did.
On the day that he arrived here, in Lexington, New York (the country, "the bush") he held counsel with his "big brother" Moussa about his condition. The two of them sitting in a small room, behind a barely closed door, inaudible. Later I asked Moussa if there was a problem, after I began to hear curious reports, and, as a good griot, keeping it private and male, Moussa replied that there was no problem. Before he made his announcement to Moussa he described to Carlos, pointing with his hands, his painful condition. "Pi pi tres chaud." Carlos then told the women; the translators, stage manager, and company manager, the ones who completely support what it is that we are doing. One woman told me and then, a week after that first meeting with Moussa, with a very descriptive sign language, he told me. He said that he wanted to see a doctor who would give him a shot

in his behind. He thinks that he caught this "sore" in New Haven. The woman that he was seeing in New Haven was described as being a "freak." He says that in Africa there is a natural remedy, herbs that one puts on the wound to heal it. I wonder what wound he means. I have also heard of an enema that Djédjé takes, preventive and weekly, made from natural plants that he flushes up his ass. "Djédjé never gets sick." This procedure makes more sense to me.

It was still light outside and Carla, the company manager, drove to another town to get his prescription. The pharmacy made a mistake and packaged a nasal spray instead. It was now dark and Carla had to go to yet another town because the first pharmacy had closed. She was lost on the road for two hours and we had to look for her with the help of the first and only black state trooper from the first town. "Let's check out the temperature of this local diner," he said as we pulled into a parking lot. At 11:00 P.M. we found Carla wandering out in front of the local police station mumbling to herself about how some laughing cowboys in a truck had run her off the road, throwing beer bottles at her minivan and shooting their guns in the air. Pacing, stunned, she said that she had seen our searching automobile many times that evening, passing her by, not seeing nor hearing her waving "stop, please stop." And then, softly breaking the recounted rescue, she wished that she "could have clearly seen the license number on that fucking pickup."
She was successful in getting the correct prescription and he only missed his evening dose.
For seven days he took an antibiotic that seemed to strip his body of any remaining defense systems. He wandered about sleeping, standing and walked without his long already ethereal legs, with eyes half cocked. Mostly he quartered in the toilet.
All the while he had a very young white college student visitor who would drive from another town, often, to visit him. They met at one of our informal performances. They would sit on top of the hill near his cabin for hours. She spoke a little French. He did most of the talking, and pointing at various simple rural circumstances. She was intrigued by his praying mantis spirit. Carlos told him that it was not a good idea for him to have sex before six weeks had passed. "This is very serious, brother." Carlos claps his hands and laughs when later telling the tale.
Two weeks later, in Brooklyn, after all the medicine was gone and he was feeling better, he got a fever. It was immediately rumored that it might be malaria. Orida, Moussa's wife, translated the rumors to me and continued into an elaboration on the cultural politics of the parasite. "While living in

America, Moussa takes a dose of paprika, simply mixed with water at the beginning of malaria season," which is April/May in Africa and maybe September/October in Brooklyn. Moussa has never had malaria but assumes, being African, it is part of his inhertitance. Orida added that if he, he being not Moussa, that "if he has malaria he will be delirious after three days." Later back in New Haven, after three days, he was not delirious. However, he is more and more solemn and weak. He stays this way, except when he dances. Then he smiles and seems to have wings.

"Ralph, I want to talk to you. I wish that we could just sit down together and talk. There are many things that I would like to say to you, in my language or yours."

He talks to me often, always with a translator and always in proverbs. "Be careful when looking down into the hole of a rat that the rat is not looking back at you."

August 26

The weather is well today. A mist over the mountains. Moussa is taking on more of a leading role, speaking out more on things that concern him. The energy of the group is as powerful as it was before. Tracie has a bad case of insomnia and seems awfully sequestered in her room with locked door day and night.

We spent what time was left after food runs and meetings reviewing the Collage phrase. It is a mess. The Africans apologized for their lack of maintenance, anything that was not hard-core rhythmic. "Back in Abidjan we were dancing another dance." Ann Carlson and Mary Ellen Strom are here with their family. It is good to see them.

Later

Yesterday started well enough and then cascaded into a Babel of sorts, a day of defining and cleaning the Collage phrase. Those many voices of what's right and what's wrong brought an added chaos of energy and focus. Still, all in all we got a lot done. James's knee is on the way out. By the end of this project he will know quite well the American medical system.

At the end of rehearsal I worked with Angelo and collaborated on a phrase that I hope will give more voice to the interesting awkwardness of translations within our shared community. Challenging the aesthetic beast. At the moment I like the work, as long as there are not public witnesses.

I worked alone later in the evening, just moving quietly in the studio. After, while walking to the large house in the damp dark, I looked for ghosts. There have been sightings here this summer. A silhouette couple, lovers, humping in the dark grass.

August 27

We split up yesterday. James, Angelo, Katherine, Rob Gorton, and I stayed in Lexington and worked on new material using the sensors, while all the others went far away to teach "darling" small kids who "didn't know their right foot from their left." An interesting proposition for modern "creative movement" but not a good thing for African dance.

The sensor work is interesting. Definitely it is a good idea but what to do with it? It could go so many ways. So far, simplicity seems to be what works best.

I'm still balking at the joy I get from this project. Fighting and I don't know why. It feels like it's not the kind of work I want to be doing any more. Essentially, this project is about dancing, which I think has had its day for me. And then there are the race issues and the "taking care of a company" dilemma. I'm not quite prepared for all of these possibilities. Katherine is teaching yoga this week and that helps a lot. Tracie has come up with some wonderful new material.

Tracie's text is
Rhythmic (African?)
Plus, it has the
Music of European
Poetry.
Can more of this
conflict be brought out?

August 28

A lec-dem in Hunter, New York. Tracie performed and is magnificent. And then we danced. The Africans, Carlos, and I each demonstrated our different methods of moving and then we performed the Collage phrase. The more I look at it the less it looks like a collage. It is primarily African, Côte d'Ivoirian, Guinean, and very entertaining. Oh well.

August 29

A lec-dem in Claverack, New York. We danced on the lawn of two-time Academy Award–winner, Ric Robbins, composer for Merchant and Ivory movies. For a moment it felt like performing on a plantation, guests sitting on blankets, eating and drinking, enjoying themselves. My first time dancing on grass. Parts of it were fun, but these past two lec-dems seem a bit glib, too easy. And the audience treats it as surefire entertainment. I have to close my eyes to what this could imply and continue investigating. I doubt that I will ever perform on an estate lawn again, especially with a group of Africans, too eerily historical. Would not have done it this time but the Africans gave the OK.

Merchant and Ivory were also there. Very down to earth. We talked about India and the dark smart people of South India. I felt silly because I had mentioned my interest in India via Geo II and had very little geographic, dance, and religious info on India to share in our conversation. Mr. Ivory seemed especially patient. Later in the evening a painter, "the hands of Picasso" in the Picasso movie told me that Merchant and Ivory basically "own India." I wonder what he means.

Today I work alone with Carlos to try to retrieve my postmodern muse.

Labor Day

The weather continues to encourage the process. The first day without Katherine. Carla left on Saturday. Orida has been a bit out of the process because of her daughter Fatou. For the next three weeks I have a smaller regulating staff. Today should be difficult. Jenny will certainly fill in.

September 2

Starting to feel the pressure again from people around the project wanting to know what's going on. Jenny says that that knowledge would help her help me and the performers want to know what it is that they are doing. Legitimate requests.

I on the other hand am feeling a little confused about how to move forward after the fine progress made during the first workshop. I have to take all that progress apart to find the path to move forward. Complicated. Or simple, if I trust that the new parts will continue to make the whole. Nevertheless, yesterday was a day of good beginnings.

September 3

We made a very interesting continuation to the Collage phrase. Falling bodies and drums. An interesting image out of all the "showtime" dancing.

But I hit a brick wall with the sensor experiment. It doesn't seem to work with the Pygmy Dance. Unless I rechoreograph it, which will take forever, and I'm becoming less and less interested in "choreography." I will try again today.

In all of this work my desire is to work with impulses that are unfamiliar to me. To challenge the logic of what I know of the dance theater world, refining the essence of whatever is coming up now, here, no matter how unusual or immediately boring. Not working for a known effect is extremely difficult.

This morning it is cold outside, the coldest that it has been since we arrived.

September 4

A very cold day yesterday. The Africans and especially Carlos were shivering throughout the day. Pam offered them another cabin with a wood-burning stove but they refused and seemed curiously apathetic to the temperature and wind. Carlos, alone and excited, accepted the invitation, gathered and carried wood into the empty cabin and started a fire, an act he says he has done every day in his winters in Virginia.

The Africans are wearing new old secondhand coats that they found at yard sales. Coats and jackets of various fabrics, bright colors, and gender styles. They seem to enjoy these new odd adornments.

After yoga Moussa demanded and led an African warm-up. Drums and full-out dancing replace the quiet and stretching that my body refuses to move without. A lot of surprises, all good. Helpful to see them unbounded.

After today I have a pretty good idea of what will work better than not within our limited time frame. Finding a precision for that which cannot be refined.

Tracie is happy but wants to write more.

Late last night I heard the voices of the performers outside my window, excited voices. I was worried that they were freezing and wanted to find shelter in the big house. They were coming back from the local bar, a very local bar. How they often spend their evenings in Africa in eighty degree temperature.

I think I have a little mouse in my wall that scratches at something every three or four hours. I wait for it to appear, into the space of my large room, changing the rhythm of its work sound but it never does.

EUROPE

September 5

Still cold. Last night I sat in Carlos's cabin, the warmest building here. He made pasta for Tracie and me. We sat and talked about our individual art sex. How we each respond to our lovers and audiences via our sexual politics. I spoke like a bigot of my curiosity toward the reigning homosexuality in my aesthetic environment.

Then Tracie and I walked back to the big house, looking at stars. I had the impression that Tracie had seen very few starlit skys in her embedded Brooklyn life.

Today we prepare for another showing. I suppose these showings (distractions) are good in that they push me toward clarity in what this work is communicating outside of my private little brain.

September 6

The Africans' focus has been questionable this week. Too many mountain spirits? The last day in the woods. I have felt very little bucolic space here. My focus and work have seemed extremely urban, survival. I suppose on some level I'm relaxing. A falling-apart paperback James Baldwin has helped my sleep.

We had a meeting yesterday and there was some discord over rehearsing today due to the showing, an "African need" to rest and prepare. This need is reasonable to me in concept but foreign in reality. I have inherited the American emasculation of work. Tomorrow we return to New York City. Not sure how much more I can experience beyond this intense journey. I must keep repeating to myself that this is an opportunity, one without expected results. And hope that I'm not tricking myself. Daily there are doors of fear. Some are fake, some are real. I imagine that I pass through them all. Time will tell.

September 8

I woke up on Sunday to the sounds of the Africans calling to each other across these fields. Sonic hoots and warbles, each describing a person and temperament. A goodbye to the hills.

They came down from their cabins carrying two empty cases of beer from their fête the night before. "Après travaille, nous sommes fête."

The drive back to the city was lovely and uneventful but there was a terrible mix-up at their New York City hotel and one or two of the performers had to sleep on the floor.

We continue.

September 9

Today we begin rehearsals at BAM.

September 10

A horrible day. It began with the Africans marching into 651's reception at the Majestic Theater wearing faces of great unease. At a later discussion it became clear that their Manhattan hotel was unacceptable. "In Africa we do not live in huts," Djédjé led. I assured them that I would solve the problem and was not aware of their housing situation beforehand, that the rooms were too small and that four of them were sharing the same room. No matter, the rest of the day was lost to this boiling-over "social problem." No concentration. Near the end of rehearsal I threatened to send everyone home but Moussa placed his hands on my shoulders and repeated, "No, no, no, it will be all right."

In the inner sanctum of Harvey Lichtenstein. On the Next Wave Festival. A collaboration between 651 Arts and BAM. Harvey and Joe have little idea what it is that I'm doing. Maurine may have a little more information. At some point next week we will show them something and I imagine them not knowing what to say, it being too late to cancel my production. Or they could find it interesting. This will be a very odd two weeks.

September 11

A better day. We all came to work a little more inspired. I tried a number of ideas that ultimately did not work. Ended the day working with Carlos on a small idea and it was very pleasant.

Met with Suzanna Tamminen of Wesleyan Press and she would like to publish my Geo. notes/writing. She would like to read more about the "performing experience," something I don't care to write about. A challenging assignment. A good suggestion. Had dinner with Tracie about text. She recommends that I work with a voice coach.

September 12

I found connective movement in the structure yesterday. And a surprising expanse of stillness and silences. I have it going on for quite a while and I wonder if it will hold and continue in context to everything else, the visual, sonic environment. Another part of my work will be directing the profound physical maleness of these performers to something softer, especially in the stares of their eyes and lips. I grew up with a particular affinity to the Negro race. That face that showed so much struggle.

September 13

Another showing, the biggest thus far. The work continues to move. I'm not so sure, forward. This much is certain: the material is very energetic and engaging. But will it be and does it need to be art?

We've been working on a section that I will call Divination: supposed foreseeing of the future. Where and how the work will probably conclude.

I now perform Map, the beginning text, standing and without the book. I now feel it in my body.

September 14

Sunday. It is four-thirty and I've just spent most of the day running errands, all Geo. related. No other life. Frustration. I had planned to write for most of the day. Now I simply want to sleep. I keep forgetting to eat.

September 15

Another showing: Judson Church. Showing unfamiliar work to a familiar audience. I look forward to the days when I can once again work without the pressure of putting what's not together together. I want again the ease of spending a whole day on something tiny. Of course, we were not about to get out of the city without some heat and after all, this Judson showing was my idea, I thought it would be fun. I'm forced to dig deeper, quicker than I feel comfortable. Some essential problems are surfacing. Better now than during previews, where more are surely paused, waiting. And critical feedback is always more audible and useful spread out during the actual building of a work. I have more to say about this but my brain just stopped working.

September 16

Last night we performed for a downtown dance audience. Fun and oddly disconcerting. Showing what we have out of context to the whole is a tricky proposition. A number of friends said that they had cried at the end of our excerpt, a section strictly within its point and involuntarily succinct. This is useful information. How do I respect that information and move forward, desiring even more tears or laughter or fear, etc.? I'll stick to my structural ideas and then, if necessary, juggle the parts.

September 17

Divination: Moussa said, "To think how to find the future. To better find the future you have to have a very elevated spirit, to think and to predict. So you know ahead where you want to go and what you need to think. It is a long road, a spiritual road, one where you can locate yourself. And one must go to the grandparents and ancestors to know what has happened before."

Angelo added, "Ambro, the sacred forest. Never forget where you come from." A day after our Judson performance we talked about differences between African and American audiences. Djédjé cited his fear with American audiences, how "they don't respond until the end and so how difficult it is to know what they are experiencing. And then they get up at the end and clap and you know that they liked it." Someone said that the audience for this work will be "hung" because they don't know where we are going.

After this long discussion we began work on a "dress dance" as part of the divination section. The material is generated from Côte d'Ivorian and Guinean women dances and a tripping-step idea, an old idea. A good beginning.

September 19
Danced for Joe Meillo, Maurine Knighton, and the staff from 651. Joe liked the drumming. There was less energy than at Judson.

September 20
James may have malaria. His eyes look like blood. I think that if he has malaria then his eyes should be yellow.

September 21
Spoke to Carlos on the telephone and he called me a "bitch." He was upset that I haven't accompanied him to a dance club to observe his underlife. He was offended that I would travel all the way to Abidjan to research the Africans but not challenge one of my precious evenings at home to examine his source of dancing. He's been asking me to accompany him since June. I have had no excuses other than having had my own American club life experience when I was younger: The Prison, The Purple Barn, Belrae Ballroom.

So, last night I went to Vinyl, on Hudson Street I was frisked at the door by a burly, friendly man. I paid seventeen dollars and another burly man taking money thanked me for attending the club. Inside it was dark with pounding music that was familiar from my past club life. The dancing was mostly black male, straight, sexual and complicated. This was unfamiliar. There were a few women either watching or moving cautiously on the edges. The mood was easy and tribal, one man in the middle of the dance floor, screaming, throughout the night. American trance. There were a surprising number of Asian (I was told Korean) wanna-be's amid the largely dark-colored bodies, who to my eyes were surprisingly smooth and playfully rhythmic. Later Carlos admitted that the scene that evening was fairly low-key. He then suggested that we go to a club that was primarily Latino and where the dancing was much more dangerous.

In his environment Carlos is unbounded, beautiful. In my context he dances in a "box," two boxes: my box and the box of the Africans, neither of which he truly understands. I resist but must bring more of his world to our process.

YOUNG APOLLO TRAVELS

He enjoyed the day that he arrived back in New Haven. Having his own apartment and the short walk to the theater. Where he has his daily clean towel for rehearsal and labeled water glass and a large production crew to entertain and complain to. Where, like all the other places in America he has been, he does not often eat because he has immediately wired his paycheck home to his mother.

There, in October he dislocated his shoulder during a rehearsal. On his back are many tiny scars, whelps. On the bottoms of his feet are many black dots covering the whole sole surface. I asked how he had done it as he curled into a protective ball. He took offense at the question as if he were being accused of lying about his pain. I did not know how to respond to that. I took him to an acupuncturist who put in a hundred needles, all over his uncomprehending body. He was terrified. I chanted "respire."

BACK IN NEW HAVEN

*There are garbage men outside my apartment window, here in New Haven,
throughout the week. The noises, vocal sounds that they make, the playful
talking, remind me of the Africans when they are outside, below my
window. Sometimes I think the garbage men are the Africans, especially
Angelo, because his voice is the most daring.*

September 23
Back in New Haven. I feel absolutely delighted to be back. There is something to be
said about working away from home. I hope my expectations of the preternatural
support of Stan, Vicky, Mark, Ben, Rich, and all, are not surprised. Our work hours
this time around are odd, 2:30 til 11:00.

September 24
Yes, there is support here but also immense pressure from the many assistants that I
have. Each assistant from the first workshop now has his or her own assistant. There
are approximately ten people behind my back at all times. Is this a potential waste?
Another goal will be finding a use for everyone.
Being back on an actual proscenium, after the privacy of walled studios, I have
questions about the stage space and all of its accoutrements. I'm basically "ghetto"
when it comes to the stage, my love of the bare and empty. Among other elements
the definition and boldness of Nari's work now threatens. I will have to get over
thinking that I'm just making a dance. Nonetheless, I have managed to make "just a
dance" with this different movement intent, and these bent-legged black male bodies,
a dance that feels oddly familiar, and somewhat pleasing.

September 25
The scope of the stage's problems versus what is simple and effective about an
informal studio is like the U.S. versus the rest of the world. So much more to
consider. Comfort and the rest of life outside the door. Yes, this period, now, feels like
I'm working with the materials of the world. I hope that this flaying is not an illusion
or denial of something less understood.
Day 3 feels like a week. Not so much in my body but in what is available, or not, to
work on. Am I obliged to make a dance for this final movement? Does "Divination"
have to be an obvious theatrical continuation? I'm thinking like a choreographer.
And that seems old-fashioned.
I'm called to dance today, perhaps tomorrow, but I suspect that something new will

fly out of this final attempt.

At times I'm embarrassed that this work has some potential direct meaning.

September 26

An interesting experiment with peripheral pause, the moments away from the directness of center stage. What to do when we are offstage and still exposed? It turned into an exercise about home. I imagined an accumulation of objects, to surround oneself, to claim a place for possessions. But the Africans once again gave another dimension to my modernist thinking. For an hour all that happened was sitting and lying on the floor and walking to another spot to visit friends and sitting and lying on the floor. My fearful eyes saw black sloth. And then we talked about how resting and lying on the earth gives a body energy and great strength, enough for "a man of sixty to work in the fields around the clock." Whenever I sleep on the earth I wake up in great pain and when I sit I prefer hard wooden chairs. I want to have a bare stage, I think because I'm afraid of saying more of abstraction than I know.

September 28

Yesterday we ran through the existing narrative for Paul Miller and all the production assistants. The space overwhelmed most of the Africans. After a month off and months in much more intimate spaces they all felt out of sync in this almost consuming theater, and the birthplace of this venture. We will have to practice filling ourselves up into this crypt. Find the size of this space again. And to complete the day's awkwardness, the sensors, Paul's input, were not working properly. Afterward Paul didn't have much to say but played a cassette of a sketch that he would like me to use, something sonically similar to Francisco's music. It could work beautifully or be redundant. I'm open to anything at this point, a new practice. He also left two DAT tapes that I've yet to hear.

Moussa asked why we were covering the drums, Nari's design, and why there were no "African costumes" in the production. I surprised myself with a very angry response and replied that I had made these choices due to expectations, ours and an audience's.

Kenny Burrell was in town for a concert. Met him while we were in Lexington. Later we went out and I told him of the discussion that I had had with Moussa and he said that we as black people are always reacting to a system that dictates these responses. I wonder if my twist on things is predicted, and part of a new societal problem, denial of soul, or of what is.

September 29

> *"What is important is not to educate but to teach the Negro not to be a slave to their archetypes." Frantz Fanon*

I spent Sunday sleeping and rereading Frantz Fanon, an energetic contradiction. His writing fires my soul and perhaps this is just what I need as this project continues to its summit.

October 1

I got an e-mail from Paul Miller commenting on his hatred of the suits that the performers rehearse in. Sweetly apologetic.

There is one tape that he has left behind that works extraordinarily well. A backward play on a string quartet. The Africans adore it.

Nari dropped in yesterday and many important problems were looked at, some solved. He confessed that as a visual artist, and given the way he has worked in the past, he has somewhat dropped this project, his design work being finished, given all the assistants and ideas fledged out on paper. He mentioned his surprise at the constant and continuing phone calls and questions. He is now living in an attic at P.S. 1 working on a very large installation about contemplation.

Today a few bottles fell and broke from the curtain in progress. Everything stopped.

October 2

Fighting a cold. Fighting a lack of ideas. The usual plight of resistance of resolution. Choreographing, which I make pressured because I'm dancing on a stage and in a town that practices Shakespeare daily.

The performers were completely undisciplined today. I told them that their actions were unacceptable and that I'd rather they go home than waste my time. They came into focus for the last half hour.

October 3

Good work yesterday. But I almost blew my knee out. I know how and where it happens and that will be very useful in pacing myself. This will be the hardest I've danced for quite a while. I can't break. I won't break. In some respects this work is an evening-length solo.

Divination proceeds well. The choreography is simple and about old, old foreigners in modern form. Confusing possibilities. Most of it works so far.

James missed yoga due to a physical therapy appointment. He wandered in at 6:00, three and a half hours later. The person that accompanied him brought him back to campus by four forty-five. She said the appointment lasted two hours. When he entered the rehearsal I acknowledged him with an angry gaze and simply pointed at my watch. He made up some untranslatable excuse. That he and time had been invisible.

October 4

Moussa is broken. He blew his knee out yesterday and was rushed to the hospital. He might be out of the work. All of a sudden I find myself regurgitating my history of directing a dance company. That the specific people placement of a work can change with a slight fall is one of the reasons that I stopped directing a company. What now? I hope to find some shocking discovery from my anxiety. And I hope Moussa recovers soon.

October 6

Today something has to happen. I demand another shift. I feel the need to be on some schedule now that there are two weeks left before previews. I could say that I just need to keep working and when I run out of time then that is all. My big concern is time. How much more time does the bottle land need to accomplish its life, after all that has come before?

I saw Moussa last night. He was walking normally. But his face looked terribly concerned. It is rumored that he refuses "to be injured." It is a fact that he left the hospital on crutches and with heavy medication in hand, both of which he threw away once back in his apartment.

October 7

Yesterday was a completely scattered day. It started with a photo shoot that went beyond the half hour allowed. I lost my patience more times than I would like to admit. Stan Pressner saw some excerpted moments. Moussa is still an unknown. At the end of the day all I could take home with me was a list of what needed to be corrected of the constructed work that is supposed to be finished, that is months old. There were no new discoveries. A break of momentum. And this final surge is all about momentum.

October 8

Today we had a lec-dem. Three hundred and fifty high school kids, the majority of them girls, screaming for Carlos. Moussa was sitting, playing drums and suddenly got up and danced. Inspiration or magic. I guess he is OK.

The two hours we worked later in the theater were good ones. What was once about trance is now about repetition, and a resolution to Divination. It should work, but I don't know if our bodies will hold up to the punishment.

We all got tickets to see Leontyne Price. Goulei asked if there would be an orchestra, with percussion. I wasn't sure and told him yes. It turned out to be a well-sung recital, Leontyne and a pianist. Djédjé, Nai, Tapé, James, and Goulei left after about thirty minutes. Angelo stayed and at the curtain call stood and sang.

October 9

Yesterday Carlos and I went to an acupuncturist, a very good one. An office in a large turn-of-the-century white house. An ex-surgeon who got fed up with the American medical way and is now sticking needles in people and very happy. It was Carlos's first time. I promised to pay for his second visit if he went the first time. I will continue to encourage the Africans to spend some of their money on body work but I don't think the very reasonable fifty dollars makes any sense to them. A continual frustration to me. I asked the Africans about their interest in a massage, the simplest of body work, which they all desperately need. Moussa and Angelo were the only ones remotely interested. Angelo said it was not an issue of money but one of reliance, that he didn't want something done to his body that his body would then learn to depend on. He told a story of his first rehearsal with Koteba, his company in Africa. How afterward he could barely walk, and did not get a massage and eventually got used to the work and the pain. Goulei said that if it were a woman that massaged him then she would have to do "more" once the massage was finished. Divination moves onward into its second part, the repetition idea, which makes thematic sense. Now, how to make it work physically in the little time left. That I began this work with an arch distrust of the African necessity for repetition and am now closing the work and hoping to find some glory in that necessity, is poetic justice to I'm not sure whom. It works. And I'll dance in the back and continue to comment on what it is that I favor: the antithesis of repetition, articulation, and "movement invention." And perhaps my particular chorus will be meaningless and that would be fine.

Moussa is OK. Definitely magic. I do believe, I do believe, I do believe.

October 10

Big discussion with my dramaturgs last night about the dialogue of Overview. This is the only moment readily identifiable to most of the Yale staff, because it's text-based, and they jump on its peculiar characteristics like a good meal. There are those that think we need to analyze meaning and those who feel that meaning is irrelevant because of the abstraction of the text. The opinion of my assistant director, a man from Israel, is that Carlos and I need to commit to a point of view, one that does not

GEOGRAPHY
Synopsis
as of 10 October 1997:jrf

TIME	EVENT	NOTES

MAP:

	ALL THREE CURTAINS IN	
0:00:00	MIDDLE CURTAIN OUT AS PLAY BEGINS	
	GOULEI/TAPÉ: SILENT TALKING	
	US CURTAIN OUT	

CRIME:

GOULEI TRIGGER "1...2...1...2...3...UH!"	Sample
RALPH: MAP TEXT	
NAI/DJÉDJÉ: PYGMY DANCE	
MOUSSA: DRUM/DANCE SOLO (TWICE)	Sample--JB note
RALPH/JAMES DUET	FL #13 Track 4 (plays out)
CARLOS/JAMES DUET	
CIRCLE DANCES W/ RALPH/CARLOS DS	
COLLAGE PHRASE WITH DRUMS	
TAPÉ: BIRD SOUNDS	
RALPH/CARLOS: OVERVIEW TEXT	FL #10 Track 2 (45 sec in)
	Both mics (FL cuts out at end)

TRIAL:

LARGE MINUET CIRCLE	
TIRE TALK	
MINUET SQUARE	
MINUET DUETS	Bach Track 1 (plays out)
GOULEI/RALPH: THROWING ROCKS	
HAIKU	US mic
JAMES/ANGELO: CLEANSING (GOWNS)	Sample--birds

DIVINATION:

SINGING ON LADDERS/BOTTLES UP	
HAIKUS	Mic DR/Mic SL
ANGELO/RALPH/MOUSSA TRIO (IN GOWNS)	
DIVINATION DANCE (IN GOWNS)	Paul Miller
MOUSSA: BACKWARDS LEAPS (CIRCLE)	
JAMES/DJÉDJÉ REPETITION	FL # 14 Track 5
MOUSSA TEXT	

falter. How would that work in a process whose very nature is to doubt? After all the voice classes and analyses, I will come full circle and let the text live its original convoluted life. But thanks to the voices and tradition of Yale I have more human science, maps to carry that life forward.

October 12
Today begins the week before everything comes together or falls apart.

October 15
A more or less complete showing last night of all the proposed parts. The running time is an hour and twenty-one minutes. A very intense work with many demanding moments, for one performer or another. Basically, it's working, but much to do before I can let go. Talked for a long time about what doesn't work with most of the assistants. The biggest problem is the Divination section. The concept of repetition is being challenged and how to choreograph it or not is the key to what it should be. It is repetition, and my deceptive way of conquering the "trance" dilemma, that somehow I want to bring an element of it to this stage. That via repetition, more repetition than they know, the performers take their dancing to a place that they and I cannot predict.
For the first time my body feels hard.

October 17
Divination II continues. James dislocated a shoulder last night and so I couldn't try one of my few options. It seems that every other day something new falls apart on his body. I'm beyond frustration and now just watch him crumble and rebound, crumble and rebound. He seems to know what he is doing. The conclusion of Divination is physically too difficult to rehearse more than once an evening. I will have to choreograph in my head and just give the performers numbers, how many repetitions and when and where they should enter, exit. It should be interesting. My body feels better today.

October 18
After a week of having what seems to be the whole of the Yale production staff as my audience, as I work through the resolution of this work, I'm about maxed out from all the feedback and my attempt at processing it. Now is the time that ideas and authority outside the process have the potential to take over. At least that is my concept of this environment. And then again it is a blessing that there is so much spoken concern/momentum to keep working, because I really want to stop, soon.
A run-through today. I still have no conclusive ideas about Divination II and the end.

THE PERFORMANCE

Preview week

October 21

Our first tech run-through. Just as Jenny called places, my left knee hinted at giving out. I danced with only my right leg. An interesting improvising. The run-through was concise structurally but the dancing was very messy. Moussa was in a bad mood that completely obliterated his dancing. James danced heroically with a dislocated shoulder. He saved his tears afterward for a corner in the back wall.

Divination moves forward. It falls apart when it tries too hard to be a modern dance; the crispness of that genre is impossible here. Divination II is close to being acceptable, for now.

I tried something at the end, after Moussa exits, a bow for three men plus a spoken word that I thought would resonate, but it came off surprisingly silly. I liked it. But it doesn't work.

October 21

Overloaded. Too much feedback about too many problems/details. The season of minutia. And now is the time when I can't empty the room. The Overview text is creating the biggest stir. My instincts say to leave it alone. It can't be what it's thought to be. Stop. The biggest problem is that Tracie can read Overview from a piece of paper, sitting down and make you cry, or at least listen. For Carlos and me, it is mostly abstract words.

The overall choreography is fragile. The tendency is for it to fall apart. And I have had too much license in working fast, and expecting unison perfection among strangers, in no time at all.

Sleep starting to pull out on me. I will have to rest in air. My body is better.

Tonight, another run-through. Stan P. is creating his usual magic light. Nari's work is gorgeous and he hasn't even seen it.

October 22

A very telling run-through last night. Mark Bly said that he's finally "surrendering to the totality of the whole." Peter was moved and noteless, very excited. Katherine continues to hold on to her perfectionist criticism, which continues to help. My own performance was low-key and not inspired. But I was impressed with the first-time whole connected scaffold. We even have a fade-out at the end. Time has run out, and now I can only refine where we are at the stop of the clock.

October 23

The official dress rehearsal. Lots of sound snafus. Otherwise it went well. I danced better but I'm still in my head, looking at what could be and is not.

Tracie is upset. Feels the text has no priority in the work and is very critical of the whole production at this moment, of her work premiering. Not sure what she means. Nari will be the collaborator who comes out the least scathed. His planted mark was nearly fully realized before I began.

October 25

On Friday we all hit pay dirt, a very good performance. The energy and pace of the show was inspiring. Still a few mechanical problems but fewer and fewer.

I feel the need to pep-talk the performers, my need to address them as these "wild" children who need to be aesthetically tamed. I wonder how much of this is more and more racism? They are all tired and I'm not finished choreographing.

The concept of "working" is taking on a new meaning. How they work and how my society overworks. What an American audience needs from theater versus what the African performers feel they need to give.

I discover their performance rituals: Moussa squeezes a lime over his legs and feet every night before going on, for protection. Nai has an elaborate gestural prayer and James kneels to the floor, touching it. Carlos and I stretch.

YOUNG APOLLO PRAYING

He premieres tonight. He wakes up and slowly limps from his bed and moves to the sink of his kitchen where he turns on the faucet and cups his hands and drinks from the palmed pool. He then moves on to the toilet and pees, holding but not looking down at his penis, focusing on his image in the mirror hanging over the toilet, the stream from his dick completely centered into the watered bowl. The toilet seat down the whole time and spotless. He moves to another room and then he sits, naked, prophetic, smoking a cigarette for a long time.

Another day he began a performance curled up into a ball, shivering with chills, under an offstage tech table. Onstage, others kept whispering to me that it was, again, possibly malaria. Throughout the first half of the performance his body shook in tiny spasms, micro-undulations, and whenever he left the stage proper he collapsed within the offstage darkness. Helped off the floor by stagehands for his next entrance. In the middle of the performance something shifted and he began to dance beyond the rest of us, as if he had not just died. After the curtain call I asked him how he was and he said "ça va." He establishes a common resurrection, more tricks from a fledgling pantheon. I am certain that it was a case of dehydration, and all the other times it must certainly be dehydration, caused by insufficient water and food.

November: Regal University Hotel, Durham, North Carolina. He was in the spa room alone, wearing a secondhand American warm-up suit, lifting weights and doing push-ups. "Pour energie," he smiled.

On the day and night of the twenty-fifth performance he wore a silver necklace with a figure of a sitting skeleton, Gautama the moment before enlightenment. He said that it was "pour le spirituel."

If he were American I would think that he had some disease. By the way his eyes do not focus and because he is so skinny, I think this because his magic has turned my seeing backward. And anyway, there is very little that I understand about being African.

I worry because there are still two weeks left for him to die.

October 27

We premiere tonight. I don't know if the problems that remain are self-induced or if there will always be a great more to excavate in this project, due to its vast polyculturalism, never allowing it to "premiere" more than what it is from day to day. The performers are pulling back, complaining about exhaustion and too much rehearsing. They want to perform what we have and leave what's left to be said unsaid, this is in great part my projection. I honestly detect resistance to detail work, especially toward the precision of group choreography, and to the moving, physicality that is new to them. I wonder how much I can push choreographic specificity and when and where do I let it be?

Another intriguing matter on stage is how they respond to the more alive system of performing versus rehearsals, the decisions that they make when there is a problem. They are all quite good. This they have perhaps mastered.

My own dancing is evolving. I can now concentrate on my work as a mover and performer. This work is a playground for all that interests me as a performer. But I'm still very emotionally ambivalent about being on stage. What the hell is my relationship to an audience? I do not know. But that essential question is clearer here, than in any other work I have performed.

Back to the Africans:

There has always been a great tension about "what is next" for them, even before we began. My moving on to another project with "other performers" after this project is over and sending them home "broken." The end of this *Geography* and the act of going home. To what? They are treated like princes here, just as they imagined. How will that change their young identities about futures and work?

October 29

Geography premieres. All the collaborators come and are surprised and happy, even Paul M., who I thought would be the most judgmental. Tracie, suddenly is thrilled. The show itself had multiple technical problems but I suppose we have it to a level where it works regardless of these seemingly minor glitches.

There was a party later and of course there was drumming and a tight circle of black sweaty men dancing and singing. Not much different from what happens onstage. Eventually the circle opened and the whole space danced.

A part of me feels as though I've done my job and can ride off into the sunset. I also know that it is only beginning. Inside and out.

October 30

Last night more of that weird emotional stuff the Africans bring to their various days. Particularly, an embrace of exhaustion, "fatigué" being a very popular word. Tapé fell asleep twice during the show, sitting on a tire seat and almost missed two cues and James just walked off alone in the middle of our curtain calls. His only excuse was "malade." I suppose this is all natural, part of what this world means in another land. This surprising performance life makes my dancing more specific, carrying the weight of what might not be there, there for me. What I have constructed here definitely wants to fall apart. "And the jungle will obliterate the shrine."

I had not expected this postpremiere responsibility. There will be no letting go of this work until they are on the plane home. Or, I suppose I could let go, and watch something else live. Now that would take courage.

Jenny is also exhausted and somewhat disappointed that she too has not arrived and finished "the beginning of a run," a place for her to relax more and enjoy consistency. Her hardest work, like mine, is just beginning.

October 31

My mammy, my mummy and daddy are here. Tonight they watch me dance for the second time in twenty-two years.

Last night the show continued its "who will forget what?" game. Goulei forgot to turn the record player on and Moussa forgets and forgets small moments and always manages to be just behind the exact time, almost perfectly. What is this forgetting? Time here is different, rest is different, attention to details are different. The other life of the work that I'm resisting, not even wanting to see. This perhaps is where I'm faking. The farce: Now that I have an audience, it seems harder to be open to the "real life" participation of these performers. I need to control exactly what of this project I want the audience to see, and close down an extremely important part of the nature of this experience. What is the nature of this control? And what is the audience really interested in seeing anyway? Certainly more than I'm showing.

> *My mother could not . . .*
> *My mother could not stop taking photographs. After meeting them, my*
> *mother says that Angelo has the most "African face." My father says that*
> *when Angelo wears his New York Yankees' cap he looks normal. But that*
> *when he takes the cap off his facial features are extraordinary. My mother*
> *liked the drumming the best. "Ralph, I was very confused until they started*
> *playing the drums and then I just had a good ol' time." She could not stop*
> *talking about Tapé's hands, how "they felt like bricks." I told her how Tapé*
> *fell asleep twice during the performance, while offstage, and how one night*

he peed in a bottle because no one is allowed to leave the stage area.

November 3

Friday night was a good show. My parents stood up and clapped at the end. My daughter Chelsea, and her best friend were also there. My mother seemed more engaged this time. Her introduction to my work two years ago left her smiling and speechless. My father was obviously pleased but had fewer questions about what he saw this time. The rest of the weekend went well. In fact, having my family/parents here relaxed and inspired me, a surprise. Two shows on Saturday that I didn't think we would survive. In fact the dancers gave one of their best performances Saturday night. Go figure.

Tapé peed in a cup or bottle while onstage. He continues to be the wild card. My own performances are somewhat forced. I'm part bored and am ready for something else. I spend my free time onstage breathing, trying to stay present.

Beginning to feel the pressure of having to do this all over again.

November 4

A company meeting, which, as usual, began a big heated discussion about various Côte d'Ivorian complaints. James blurted that all I care about is my show, not their problems. He is almost right. I was trashed the rest of the evening. A complement to my already suspicious anger.

The show was solid with a few minor problems. Angelo, who was the most dependable body during the building process is now consistently dropping moments during Divination. I think it is due to the immense pain in his lower back. My dancing was uninspired and then the zipper on my dress broke. I went home deeply depressed about my stage life. And my left deltoid is distressed.

Tonight we videotape. I can't imagine this work living a longer life in the performing arts library, having a life that one can look at repeatedly. Not knowing so much of this work is embarrassing. Now there is something to brag about.

November 6

Two shows today. And the performers are starting to become heroic. I continue to make adjustments, subtle changes, that work from my inside. But I'm not sure how well they work from the front of the theater.

November 8

I've been in severe pain for a couple of days. A pulled, strained something in my left shoulder. Kelly visits every other weekend and practices acupuncture, covering my back and knees with needles, helping me stay upright. I sleep through most of her treatment, falling in love with her again. And every other body in this show is disguising an injury of some magnitude. Angelo doesn't do our yoga warm up because of his back and instead runs up and down a small stairwell to warm-up. The show goes on. Mythic black tolerance? James was delirious onstage last night, beginning the show curled up under the stage left tech table. Orida said that he mentioned feeling the beginning effects of malaria, again. While on stage Moussa kept whispering to me every chance he could that James was very sick. James kept dancing. And at one point when he and I stand next to each other I felt him shivering and prepared myself for some on the spot partnering. Suddenly he was fine. And finished the show dancing like a superforce. He went home and took some "African herbs." At least four bodies were limping after the curtain calls. The show is getting tighter. I'm a nervous wreck. No more anger, though; now I'm just surviving. In fact, my performances are starting to let go. I'm finding another place to focus and work, with less resistance. My body wants to hold me back but not enough to completely debilitate my desire to keep moving forward. This is encouraging. I wonder what the others are feeling?

November 10

End of the Yale run. Some reviews: "during the dull moments, which are considerable, one can look at the rich set." "Lemon's uneven geography exhilarates and exasperates." Misunderstood or not understood. I'm prepared for it, somewhat. I embrace that my work does what it has to do, for me and my audience. There is the

reality that for my audience it might not do much. A possible casualty of my self-involved abstraction, hermeticism. I wonder about those voices that stay integral to a difficult vision and are able to communicate brilliantly to an audience, a general one. But what is a general audience and how many of "those voices" are out there? It is certain that difficult work takes time, if ever, to convince someone/anyone of its relevance outside of itself. Fact. So, I'm patient and more to the point, persistent in my need and truth to do what it is I have to do, no more but absolutely all that is.

The last couple of performances were eventful. A powerfully normal matinee. In the evening I felt angry and impatient. Something to do with letting go and being tired and fed up with the daily preparation, revealing, and uncertainty. The performers were tired and wonderful.

I sat in the theater with Stan W. and watched them strike the set. A famous strike. Especially the casing of the bottles. Rich Gold is mythical. As we left the building we stopped to talk to the truck drivers, one of them, a lady from New Zealand, LuAnn, who lives in Indiana with her driving partner and husband. I told her to please take care driving because her cargo was eleven hundred bottles.
Less than twenty-four hours at home. Confusing. Kelly is a welcome sight.
In the air to Minneapolis, hometown. That's as far as I am.

THE TOUR

November 11

A talk/video showing at the Walker last night. Small audience. I don't know if I know anyone here any more.

> *A dream*
> *That same old opera house with the six flights of stairway that wander up the back of the theater. I cannot find part of my costume and I have missed my first and or second entrance. Still I have to run downstairs to enter for what's left. I have friends in the audience whom I have forgotten to assign complimentary tickets to. I'm trying to figure out what to say to them afterward.*

November 13

The guys are in fine moods. And unruly. James and Moussa got into a big screaming fight while rehearsing Collage. The movement of Collage is made up primarily of Côte d'Ivorian movement, small, concise, and quick. Moussa has voiced concern from the beginning that his larger, more expansive Guinean movement was not fully represented and that the Côte d'Ivorian movement felt like "steps for roaches." James ranted back, defending his country until he could no longer dance, sitting out the rest of the rehearsal.
I love these smaller steps, an African dancing I had never seen before.
Yesterday Moussa and Djédjé cleansed the space of the State Theater, a huge turn-of-the-century vaudeville house, singing prayers, the likes of which the State's ghosts have never heard.

November 16

On Saturday Angelo announced that he was being made a fool of by the Ralph Lemon Company, because he was not teaching in Durham or Austin. That he had not been notified of the addition of classes that Moussa and Djédjé were teaching. What followed was a very tense issue between him and Moussa. Later he and Moussa hugged and laughed. The Africans have a way of firing up a subject and then dropping it with laughter, abandoning all the "in charge Americans," leaving us behind, feeling defeated. Carlos is continually perplexed with his "motherland big brothers."

Sunday. Minneapolis. departure. This morning my body hurts.
State theater last night: Took the essential hot shower before the performance. Djédjé was in the next stall. He sang a very powerful dirge. I sang along.
Almost filled the house. But we didn't completely inhabit the space. A fairly smooth

show, with lots of bugs and snags. My dancing was very full. Tapé's djembe skin split in the middle of his solo. He literally threw the broken drum off stage, grabbed another drum and continued playing more furiously than before. In that small pause no music was missed. Four skins broken in the week due to the cold. The bottle curtains got caught and didn't finish. Standing ovation. Many old friends. Laurie Carlos said that the work was "brilliant and too long." My Aunt Barb and cousins were polite. I felt dismal, depressed. I wanted to give a better, flawless show for my hometown and didn't know it. We had an hour to tech a work that had two weeks to tech and preview at Yale. We are starting over on tour. And the work will undoubtedly be compromised for these four performances. Old frustrations. From here on in I've decided to fly the bottle legs in instead of flying them up. I can't bear the low percentage of them working properly from their original piles on the floor. James is glad to leave the beautiful cold of Minneapolis. His brittle bones still shaking.

The truck and set have thirty hours to get to Durham.

November 17

North Carolina is still changing its leaves. All that's left of fall. This morning James was lifting weights "for energy" in the spa room. Angelo walked in at one point and strutted and then walked out of the room flexing, displaying all the work that he had done in the previous city's Holiday Inn spa room.

The drummers have a big day today. Stretching and the putting on of three new skins.

Carlos and Moussa have classes. Hip-hop and Guinean. Carlos is frustrated with the turnout in his previous classes and with the more popular reception to West African dance. He wants to try to combine the classes so that students can more readily see the connection between hip-hop and African dance and not perceive hip-hop as something marginally American urban. He prefers the description "urban house styles." A politically smart idea. Carlos continues to find beautiful black women everywhere we go.

I had an interview today and the interviewing student informed me that there was some racial tension on campus and asked if I thought that *Geo.* might remedy some of the tension. I said no. In fact, it might incite because it explains or suggests absolutely nothing.

Large rocks thrown
unto the steel door
amplified, while other
movement is happening.
what about bottles?
(CRIME)

PARADISE
PARADIS
LAGO ↙
Guinea
Cote d'Ivoire
Virginia
Ohio
Mammy
Mammy
Mammy
Mammy
que bleu

Later some one is
actually lined up
against the wall
to be executed?

ALVIN AILEY DANCING REVELATIONS

I've been thinking a lot about rage.
One night I was at the Wall of Rocks and something came over me. I
stopped in the middle of the choreography, the specific moving from one
side of the wall to the other, and stood, with my back to the audience
pounding away at the wall. I lost the timing and music of the work and was
experiencing something quite new, unstructured, satisfying, and uncaring. I
stopped when I heard the sound cue that begins the next section.
I wonder often about the differences between the rage of the black American
male and the rage of the African male. The Africans find America very
violent but we have never had the violent atrocities in this country that
nearly all of Africa has experienced. Perhaps we are too young and haven't
had the opportunity. When I was in Africa I experienced a psychological
violence that frightened me more than anything I've experienced at home.
Mostly my projection of aggression, toward only African men, who wanted
to get into my thoughts and pockets, to talk and to bargain, to exist,
basically with who I was there, to them.

November 20

Austin, Texas. Seventy-five degrees. I'm happy because of the sun. A class in a giant arch-windowed studio from the thirties. Like "Doris Humphrey and wanting to dance." Lots of light. A class with a group of students from beginning to beginning. Those eyes that don't quite focus or that focus too much. I spoke of "claiming the fool" and "the embrace of embarrassment. Dance like hell as you stumble to find unanswerable questions." Students still wear tights.

Duke was good. A giant stage. Found new zones for aging parts. The bottles flew in instead of tangling up, perfect form but I miss the noise the bottles make. Another night where the drumming was not so inspired as it could be. The drum heads are better but Tapé's hands are busted, bleeding. The dancing continues to get better, oddly. In my own body I'm nightly looking for pedestrian reasons to move in the ways that I'm moving. Barely successful.

At a radio interview Moussa and Angelo sang a song from the Circle Dance section in Satellites, a slower version, more soulful, unplugged. The radio man asked a number of exotic questions and I left him to his ignorance, pretending that he was smarter than most. Moussa and Angelo had no problem with any request for a display of their African talent.

It is rumored that James has run out of money and has not been eating for the past few days. I can tell because his eyes look like pools of mud.

November 22

First Austin performance: One of the best. A smaller space and more physically intense. More rage. I hit the steel wall as if I were retaliating for all past indiscretions. More and more freedom in my old body and it hurts. My body will just make it. A class and one more performance and then two weeks off to lick my wounds.

A party at Ann Daly's the night before. The Africans danced all night on her patio, how they talk to each other. Much of their actual talking is laughter. Djédjé said to me that he feels very bad when he thinks of the end of *Geography*. Tears in his eyes. And then tears in my eyes.

Tonight James asked me for five dollars. I wanted to give him ten but Orida said not to, that she had been giving him money already.

When in a good mood Djédjé has begun to pray in English, "God is good, God is fat."

November 24

The final performance in Austin, and the twenty-fifth performance overall, went well. Too well, perhaps. The audience laughed and applauded throughout. New to this work. Deborah Hay said it sounded like a circus, distracting. I'm not sure. Someone is responding to what I have directed; it just so happens that I have not directed for any particular emotional response. For the first time in my life I have numbers of black people talking to me about my work, mostly black women. Black men, however have not really been present. I have heard, always from black women, that some black men are insulted, angered, and perplexed over the gowns, wondering why I have emasculated these powerful black men by putting them in dresses. Some black women have found the gowns powerful and beautiful. My mother and father have said nothing to me about the gowns.

My control of this work and the performers continues to be challenged. James and Moussa began laughing near the end of Tire Talk, because James had earlier grabbed Carlos under his standing seat. Carlos was furious. The rest of the performers sat through the silent part of Tire Talk, imploding with the need to laugh. James ran off stage afterward collapsing to the floor, hysterical, missing his next entrance. I wanted to fire him, and Moussa, because they could not control what was truly funny. I held my own laughter because I wanted the audience to see how serious my work is. Alone again.

My body is trashed and I'm very very tired. A friend said that I grabbed my back, painfully, during my solo. News to me.

Back to New York. It is good to be home.

Repose 2

*On Thanksgiving they went to Brooklyn and Orida made them turkey and
rice and vegetables. In fifteen minutes everything was gone. "They are so
hungry. They must be saving their money." They know something that we
don't. Moussa does not understand how there can be a Thanksgiving and a
decimation of the Native American culture existing at the same time and
place. Later they went down to the basement and played on Orida's drum
machine and danced and sang.*

*I have not seen them for a week. I did not want to. I hope that they do not
think that I have abandoned them. I cannot really talk to them outside of
work so I bet that all of us think that it is OK.*

*When we got back together after a week we were all very happy to see each
other.*

December 3

Two days back. Re-rehearsing. Without Carlos and Moussa. I was sick for the the first
two days. Same stressed stomach condition like all the other reentries. Dancing in
New York has always been more trial than ease. The guys are rested, smiling and
excited, although Angelo lies on the floor as often as possible (I assume due to his
back pain). James, between laughing and "floating," caresses his right hip injury. My
body is better but there are places that I also caress. I continue to refine and shape
what else might be in this odd work. The strangest means of choreography I've ever
tried to process. We are refining. Editing apologies. The most successful attempt at
this act/concept that I have experienced thus far. Absurd that we should still be
making fundamental changes this far into this project and with three more
performances before it's all over. To my surprise, they are just as interested in the
cleaning idea at this point as I am, but we are all deeply tired and it becomes a
problem of energy—and for some, most likely, eating.

December 5

Yesterday Moussa and Carlos returned. We are all here. And that energy has
obliterated the quiet of the three days before. They show their moods so passionately.
Moussa decided that he wanted to rehearse in his fashionable but very large, bulky
snow boots. Angelo, for the second day in a row, complained about not having a
towel at rehearsal. What was he "to do with his sweating?" He was very serious.
I'm still making changes, more text, singing stuff, oddly enough. And adding drums
to Overview. A questionable addition.

Heard that we have the whole front page of the Sunday *New York Times*'s Arts and Leisure section. At first this angered me. I don't want the expectations that go along with that kind of publicity. And then many hours later I decided that there were other things to be distracted by, like one final lec-dem today, which feels completely after the fact. There's very little left to talk about and what we have to show is now married to the stage and Nari's bottle and dead bed world.

December 8
A very unruly day. The guys had Jenny in tears. A disagreement with the rehearsal schedule. Too many hours. They are concerned about their energy.

Lecture-demonstration at NYU. A little after the fact but it went well and was fun. Nice to have questions from students of dance.
Moussa is very upset because his photo has not been in any of the preview periodicals. The Sunday *New York Times*'s article was the final catalyst. He said to me that he doesn't know what he will have to take away with him after *Geo.* is over. He said a photo would prove to his family and friends that he was there. All the (English) words in the hordes of publicity that we have received are irrelevant to his African and American community.
The following day Moussa was processing his disappointment and useless in rehearsal. I hope he figures it out before Wednesday, opening night.

To write the Times *article Ann Daly interviewed me for a year. At the last interview she asked for my reading list during the past year and a half:*

The Oresteia, Aeschylus
The Greek Myths, Robert Graves
Cosmopolis, Stephen Toulmin
Faces of the Gods, Leslie G. Desmangles
Darwin's Athletes, John Hoberman
Of Water and the Spirit, Malidoma Patrice Somé
Out of America, Keith B. Richburg
The Heinemann Book of African Poetry in English
The Wretched of the Earth, Frantz Fanon
The Autobiography of My Mother, Jamaica Kincaid
Giovanni's Room, James Baldwin
Orchard Keeper, Cormac McCarthy
Child of God, Cormac McCarthy

Outer Dark, Cormac McCarthy
Purple America, Rick Moody
Lamb at the Altar, Deborah Hay
Pussy, King of the Pirates, Kathy Acker
The Lesson of the Master, Henry James
Shot in the Heart, Mikal Gilmore

Rereadings:
Black Skin White Mask, Frantz Fanon
Cane, Jean Toomer
Things Fall Apart, Chinua Achebe
The Dead, James Joyce
Absalom, Absalom, William Faulkner
Swann's Way, Marcel Proust
Tao Te Ching, Lao Tsu

December 10

Monday. A good day. Everyone was light and expectant. A right energy for BAM. I
tried some African steps today and my knees buckled after thirty seconds.
Exhilarating and then stupid. Tracie brought changes for Overview. Crisper. We will
try Tapé on djembe for the first part of it. Carlos hates the idea. He likes our solitude.
So do I. But this experiment will give Tracie's work a truer voice.
Walked over to the Majestic. Everyone is excited. Should be a good run, if my knee
behaves. All the other performers are hurting and putting up.

December 11

Opening night. A good show. In attendance were delegates from the U.N. The
Assistant General read something about racial tolerance from the pen of Secretary
General Koffi Annan. A few minor mishaps but a very fine opening night. A funny
moment: Angelo forgot to take his pants off under his dress during Cleansing and
noticed this unacceptable costume midway through. He slowly walked off and James
did the remainder of Cleansing as a solo. Angelo was angry throughout the rest of the
evening; he said that it "messed" up his head. But I managed to make it laughable to
everyone else in the dressing room at the end of the night—everyone except Angelo.
Harvey Lichentenstein came backstage to congratulate everybody. He seemed pleased.
The Africans didn't know who he was, even after introductions.

December 13

Last night was a great show. Every moment clicked. My best Map to date. I felt a certain comfort with the lights and the space. The company's dancing energy was inspired, extravagant, but did not break my structured boundaries. Tire Talk was perfect. My dancing was spacey, almost delirious. The one flaw was the bottles flying in, musically uneven.

Afterward there were far too many folks wanting to say hello. Awkward.

Went to Juniors with more of my family and had a hamburger. One more show.

December 14

A very emotional final performance. The evening was tight with a few immaculate mishaps: I completely lost my focus in Satellites. Goulei broke his djembe skin during the Divination duet and Moussa beautifully deconstructed the final text, losing himself in the final minutes.

The bows were full of tears and hugging, especially the KiYi men. And then a rush to the dressing rooms and showers to cry some more. Except for Goulei who sat in a corner, with eyes red and wet as dark rain.

Now that I think about it, it seems odd that there is not a pause here, a space where we spend time together not rehearsing or performing. Some arrangement of living (sharing) another magnitude of our lives. There is one day between this end and everyone going home for good. A sleight of hand.

December 16

We met at the Off Soho suites on Monday morning. Tapé and Goulei were in the middle of the lobby packing up last-minute bags and bags. Tapé was also changing his clothes and shoes, at one point stripping down to only a pair of shorts. James was sitting in a corner, quiet as usual, smoking. Djédjé and Nai came down later, smiling. There were no drums. They were leaving all of them behind in order to transport newly acquired giant cases of clothes, basketball shoes, and substantial electronics, including a disco ball.

There was no Angelo. We were told that Angelo would meet us at the airport, that a friend of his had picked him up earlier because Angelo had to travel to the airport in time to freight his bicycle and some other large objects.

The airport

At the airport we stood at the ticket counter for two and a half hours while Djédjé, Nai, Tapé, and Goulei shuffled items from one excess weighted bag to another emptier piece of luggage. The whole time screaming at Orida that they travel all the time and that this is not the way they are used to traveling. "What is the problem? These bags should be accepted. We bought them here. What is the problem?" In the beginning there was a ticket clerk of African descent who knew our situation the moment we hauled the heavy bags up to his counter. Immediately flustered, and perhaps embarrassed, he asked a superior to be relieved, complaining about the time that our group was going to take. He was replaced by a woman of Haitian descent who appeared to have all the time in the world. The Africans took all the time that she gave and approximately three counters of space. There was a growing crowd of others waiting for us to finish.

Throughout this remarkable maze, Jenny, Tracie, and I watched, commented and waited. I was neither embarrassed nor impatient. One big step removed from certain fears, and now I found the piles and noise of chaos exotic. They were foreigners again, going home.

At some point during the melee James quietly walked away to have a cigarette. We winnowed the extra freight cost down to eight hundred dollars for nineteen pieces of oversized luggage. We split the cost. (At that final goodbye they could have asked for anything and I would have given it, except for money. Because money was too easy to lie about.) James never came back. And then it was clear that Angelo was never going to show up.

We put everyone else on the plane. They seemed excited about going home. They told me not to worry about Angelo and James, that they were professionals and had traveled to many places and were probably already on the plane.

There was not a delay of the flight because of the two missing passengers.

YOUNG APOLLO DRESSES UP

The weather is getting colder. He wears layers of sweaters and nylon hooded windbreakers adorned with numbers and letters spread out into cryptic gardens. I no longer ask about his health. I no longer look for physical complaints but sometimes I see him caress a part of his anatomy, familiar parts that disrupt his last few rehearsals.
During the final week of our project a woman flew from Minneapolis to New York City to visit him, someone he had met two weeks earlier on tour. She did not speak French and did not stay for the final performances. During the dress rehearsal he saw me drinking a golden liquid, a health drink of ginseng and electrolytes, and politely asked if I would bring him one for each performance night. His dancing during the final performances was flawless.

On the day of his departure home he sat in the lobby of the hotel, quiet, nervous, hiding some secret in his long caving spine. We shook hands. He asked me to write my name, address, and phone number into his tiny address book. He opened it to a random blank space.
At the airport he left the group early on, walking away to go outside to have a cigarette. He caught my eye and smiled, pointing to the outside while waving his cigarette. "You always have to throw yourself into the water." He never came back. The plane was not delayed.

I imagine him somewhere in Brooklyn, sad, because he misses his mother. He said many times before that he misses his mother, who is alone and not well. He has until December 25 to get married.
I told the airport story to a foreign friend. "Americans are so naive."

PROTEUS

What I choose to remember from the beginning or something else I stole from the *Oresteia*:

These have no wings, I looked but black they are, and so dauntless. Their heavy breathing echoing makes me cower. And their eyes fire a discharge, yellow sweet. Their hair the roots of sacred trees, or the crowns of glowing bushes. And what they wear—to flaunt that at the gods, the idols, deft, poetic cloth that smells like earth, reverent! The original tribes that produced that brood I never saw, will never see or a plot of ground to boast it nursed their kind without some tears, some perfect pain for all its labour. Suffering into truth. I found a part of it that is mine. Because that is what I wanted to see.

Back to the world of faith, in the back seat of a taxi, homebound, feeling less civilized than before. Wondering where the escapees sat, those that got it, and to the end, annihilated what was left of any imposed structure. Certainly not flying to their kingdom deep in the great ballroom of the earth. And too soon into a reality not sheltered by the stage. They would now become every other young modern American dark man, apprenticing underground with the help of seasoned friends, "free." Just like their free American "baby goat" from Virginia, and their "big brother" living in Brooklyn. But not like me. I am somewhat guilty. My proposals of power: A refined shower, white painted walls, a refrigerator, pizza, bicycles, keys. Their clothes began to flout like mine. A new generation spoiled into false liberation. Because "the modern African is forced out of Africa, on airplanes, to look for survival in America, because black Americans are rich, rich, rich." I am even guilty about those who return to sovereignty and prophesying. Dreaming that "someday there will be no reason to run away from a homeland where mothers suck the snot from their babies' noses." But my guilt is powerless and eventually I will black them all out. Those that were smiling, those that would not look me in the eye.

I imagine that they are all afraid that I will never speak to them again. That is not an option. I never really spoke to, had a conversation with any of them beyond my attempts at manipulation, collusion into the death plan of my theater. A particular aesthetic matricide. My soft commands to avenge my ambivalent heart. I had no other useful language. With one exception: As a group we made up a language about making love, one we used all the time, because it was necessary to all of us, and our one universal connection where none of us were confused. Certainly, when we danced we communicated, but basically we left one another alone. A manhood thing, but colorful in spite of itself.

I have said this many times: I brought them over mightily, engaging their color as a material from which to manipulate, like cobalt or ebony. Source material to my own prescribed history. An art project. When they arrived, race was the furthest thing from their lives. Imagine, a giant continent that has never been anything but black. A cancellation of race, no matter how many times foreigners have gone there for farming, sex, and murder. They came to America and, to my surprise, I was heralded into a world of grace and divination, color-blind. They came as dextrous, lyric missioners from their complicated forever land. And brought with them hundreds of drums, their spiritual commodity, and a prayer at every turn. Every day I felt tricked. It is still riotous in my ear. "God is good, God is fat."

We spent hour upon hour ambitiously offering our fates to one another. Proving how good we all were at what we did best. Quietly debating whose style was closer to the truth. And then we moved into territory that was new and then did what we do best in that meta-constructed environment. The most moving part was watching it fall apart. My born-again surrender to "fucking it up." That was all that I could direct, because that is what I finally realized was the point to all of it. What I had learned from them, what they had been doing from day 1, choicelessly living their truth, that form is most alive at its precipice. Even onstage, especially in front of witnesses, the performance and performers continued to break apart daily into pan-relevant transformations, recycling every act. And I began to close my eyes so that I could simply stay relevant, not alone. There would be no "trademark." On and on.

And then one day their chorus: "We have no more inspiration to give you. It is time to stop. Time to go home."

No one moving, but all of them standing, looking at me, with eyes truly finished. At the end we embraced one another fresh from theatrical bloodshed. Navels exposed. Completely naked or wrapped in white towels. Cried. Always suspicious. Our act of recognition. At least I did not destroy my flesh and blood. In fact, my body was moving better than ever before in between the spasms and pain. And kept admiring how powerful everyone else was without definition, within the world of "performance or nothing," that one hour after it was all over they could have easily been stepped on like insects, could later walk the streets and no one would care, and could get away with it. So, so what if "Huck Finn" were black?

Did this rite tame our wildness, my cultural paradigm? No, we were never wild, just feral. They were themselves. I could not embody their energy; my knees would scream, not allow it. I danced enduring, what I have always danced. To them, my

experimentation was basic, like eating a food that makes you shit differently.
Did this rite give each of us more national purpose? (For the moment let's forget
about race.) Yes, we will always be from different places. And either way a crisis. No
one changed his or her life, just the environments around us.

So back to the world of renunciation.
Looking out the taxi window I watched a woman on a corner stopped by a man with
a piece of paper in his hands, pointing here and there, apparently asking for
directions. Once, many years ago, I was stopped by a woman, with an island accent
and a piece of paper in her hand, who said she was lost and had had all of her money
stolen. The story grew and two hours later she stood in my apartment holding on to
my television set, which I had just handed her, so that she would "trust" me, my help.
Later I discovered that there were also two hundred dollars and my great-grandfather's
gold watch missing from my secret hiding place. I thought that I had had my eyes on
her the whole time.
Didn't keep my eyes on Tapé, Goulei, Djédjé, Angelo, James, Carlos, Moussa, Nai,
because the less I knew the more mystery I would have to work with. I was the one
flailing my arms, asking for directions. And at the end nothing was missed but wives,
mothers, and children. And time away from primitive rituals.
Time away from my primitive ritual. I asked the driver to stop the car, to drop me off,
somewhere where I could hear Brahms or Beethoven, a capriccio or sonata. Knowing
that I needed that sound, the passivity of it, and that I would listen differently.

Four weeks later I received two messages on my phone machine, one from Africa, in
both African French and broken English and the other from somewhere in Minnesota,
in a newer English than I had ever heard. Neither left instructions nor purposes.
They have always lived beyond my democratic concerns and are already apparitions.
"Presence is compared to absence," Angelo said. And I said, "I am not in love." But I
feel something just as useful, referential. For a moment, at that crack in my world, I
admired, adored every feature. I too want to survive. There is no younger or older
Orestes. I tried simply to humanize both worlds. My acquittal, and that brief portion
of time where we would be torn apart.

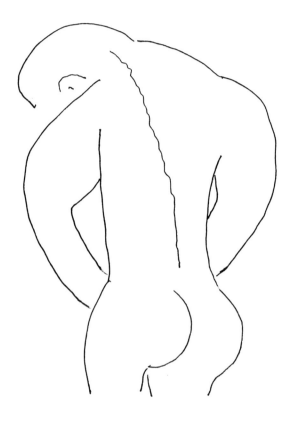

the common spine

EPILOGUE

Ralph:

I'm in no hurry to return to Africa.

Leader:

Was it not beautiful there? Did it not make you proud?

Ralph:

Ah, beauty! Yes, in how beauty is dangerous. I'm proud of that.

Leader:

And what did you do with that danger? Was something destroyed? If so it would be news to us.

Ralph:

I'm not sure. My intentions were mixed. Besides, they're gone and I've heard no news.

Leader:

Why did you do any of this in the first place? Who persuaded you?

Ralph:

The idea came at a time when I was defenseless. It was my own.

Leader:

Was the peril from before not enough? Your art somehow cursed, cast out?

Ralph:

It was enough. But now I've done this.

Leader:

And?

Ralph:

Gotta know where you come from, otherwise you'll wander forever.

Leader:
And?

Ralph:
Thinking about when I'll have to go back. That's all.

October 27, 1999.

Autumn in New York. The Yankees just won the World Series. Swept the Braves. Atlanta weeps. Four Africans from *Geography* now live in the U.S. Illegally. Vermont, Maryland, Minnesota, New York, I have heard.

I lectured recently at California Institute of the Arts in Los Angeles and shared with students my complex concern that the project of *Geography*, for all of its excitement, was also extremely disruptive to the lives of the performers that I introduced to my performance culture, my very different world. An exchange student from South Africa, a young woman, white, came up to me afterward, "Yes, I know exactly how those African men felt, how exciting it is here in America, so modern, very sexy, yes, I love it too, it's so great, I want to live here."

OR

November 13, 1999

A dream

A beach in Brooklyn. The indoor Japanese kind. Small, illusory. In bathing suits lying on beach towels on fake sand over concrete are the African performers from *Geography*, a few of them. I see Kouakou Yao Angelo curled up asleep nearest the water. There is also a bright fake sun. I walked over to Djeli Moussa Diabaté lying farther away from the fake ocean, wearing sunglasses, no other generalized accoutrements, no radio, books, magazines. He turns away, angry, jilted. (He and I have not talked since Fall of '97.) His family, Orida and the kids, Bijou and Fatou, are on another towel closer to Akpa Yves Didier James and to the water. They seem happy, playful.

GEOGRAPHY

Performance Text by Tracie Morris
Photographs by T. Charles Erickson

- How many languages do you speak? How do you feel about each one? What do most people in your family/town/circle speak?
- When do you speak each language?
- Do you feel you have a mission in life? If so, how do you know? If not, what do you think you'll probably be doing for the rest of it?
- What is your religion? Does your family practice it? If not, why not? If so, for how long?
- In what ways do the traditional and contemporary mix in your area? In other parts of Africa you know about?
- Have you travelled outside of your area much? If so, what differences did you like most? Dislike most? Thought were similar to your area?
- What do they think are the unique features of modern Africa?
- What are the major differences you see within Africa? Major similarities throughout Africa?
- What does/would unify the continent?
- Do you see anything in common overall among Black people outside of Africa? Black people including Africa?
- What is the general perception of African Americans?
- What makes them believe or disbelieve these perceptions?
- What, if anything, do you think is wrong with Black Americans? What, if anything, do you think is good?
- If the person is in a more traditional environment with an emphasis on oral history, how do the stories in their area deal with slavery and the de-population of Africa?
- What do you think will happen when you come to the U.S.?
- Name something that you would never discuss in detail with an outsider?
- Who do you consider outsiders?
- Describe, in detail, something that you love to do
- What are your favorite sound? (whatever this may mean)
- Tell the best story you know. (It can have music or not.)

(P. S.: These questions are not necessarily in order. RL should decide)

Characterizations for Geography

Carlos = young Ralph/Ralph's muse
Moussa = Older Ralph, griot, secure
Ralph = Ralph in flux
Angelo = The synthesis of the above three

Dje Dje = Ralph in Africa
Nai = Dje Dje's accompanist
James = Ralph's guardian angel
Goulei = Ralph's ancestor
Tape = Ralph's boyhood/freedom

==

Organization

Map - Vignettes to establish the world

       Tape and Goulei - dissension in heaven
       Ralph's solo text - establishes his placement now.
       Moussa - establishing his Self (power dynamics. the politics implicit in Geography)

Crime - Contrasts within the world

       Circle dance - beauty of the world
       Collage with drums
       Goulei's haiku
       Minuet

OVERVIEW - THE BRIDGE

Trial - Attempts to resolve contrast

       Rock throwing - demonstrating what's wrong
       tire talk - acknowledging the problem. trying to work it out
       endurance is the trial playing itself out.

Divination - Divine intervention and resolution

       haiku and bottles - raising/ invoking the dead
       Moussa - peace, introspection

Hi Sen & Ann —
xtra copy R.L. wanted?

MAP SECTION

VOCAL INTRO

womb womb womb womb womb womb womb womb womb womb womb womb womb
womb womb womb womb womb womb womb womb womb womb womb womb womb
womb womb womb womb womb womb womb womb womb womb womb womb womb
womb womb womb womb womb womb womb womb womb womb womb womb womb
womb womb womb womb womb womb womb womb womb womb womb womb womb
womb womb womb womb womb womb womb womb womb womb womb womb womb

more more more   more more more more more more more more more more
more more more more more more more more more more more more more
more more more more more more more more more more more more more
more more more more more more more more more more more more more
more more more more more more more more more more more more more
more more more more more more more more more more more more more

room room room room room room room room room room room room room
room room room room room room room room room room room room room
room room room room room room room room room room room room room
room room room room room room room room room room room room room
room room room room room room room room room room room room room
room room room room, room room room room room room room room room
room room room room room room room room room room room room room
room room room room room room room room room room room room room

my mummy my mummy my man my mammy my   mummy my man/MY MAMMY MY
MUMMY MY MAN my mammy my mummy my man/my mammy my mummy my man/my
mammy my mummy my man/my mammy my   mummy my man/my mammy my mummy
my   man/my man may man my man my   man my man my/man my man my man
my

map map MAP MAP map map MAP MAP map map MAP MAP map map MAP MAP
map map MAP MAP map map MAP MAP map map MAP MAP map map MAP MAP
map map MAP MAP map map MAP MAP map map MAP MAP map map MAP MAP

Dje Dje and Nai duet
(overview intro. in Bete and French with additions in English)

Mene Mene etc. (sentence)	
Many, many	
Mene etc. (sentence)	
Many of us	
Mene etc. (sentence)	
found ourselves, found ourselves lost.	
I am supposed to be I am supposed to be I am supposed to be	Noh Noh, Noh Noh
The lead in	Dans ce Dans ce paradis
Ki Yi - K Ki Yi - K Ki Yi - K Ki Yi - K Ki Yi - K	 comme l'enfer
- Os?	
But. I ah	Noh Noh, Noh
I - A - Kuko A cool/cool/cool kuko	
The lead Cool so	Back, Bock Back, Bock
Teeth on edge	eje, eje
Tre chaud	sho' nuf
show show	sho' nuf sho' nuf
chaud chaud	
	eau.

170

'Kid Song' (sound poem icw with <u>Crime Section</u>. - maybe icw Paul's 'alarms?')

bishoop   bishoop bishoop b-bish-bishoop
                                    b-bish-bishoop

bishoop   b-bish-bish

(1x)

bishoop   bishoop bishoop b-bish-bishoop
                                    b-bish-bishoop

bishoop   b-bish-bish

(repeat)

doonk - chicka - chicka - doon - doon - chick
doonk - doonk- doonk .
chicka - doonk - doon - doon - chicka -
doon - doon - chicka - doonk - doonk.

doonk - chicka - chicka - doon - doon - chick
doonk - doonk- doonk .
chicka - doonk - doon - doon - chicka -
doon - doon - chicka - doonk - doonk.

doonk - chicka - chicka - doon - doon - chick
doonk - doonk- doonk .
chicka - doonk - doon - doon - chicka -
doon - doon - chicka - doonk - doonk.

Ralph   ¹¹   PALPH
                              OVERVIEW   L

In this
In this heaven
in this heaven   *Carlos*
like
hell

we affirm an inverted   invented
God

this is either a void   to avoid
or blinding light   blinding

either way i see nought   drought
but blue   blues

indominable

A straight   streak
creek   flash
sinew of haze

I am green   green with
a   know   green with
a   know   greenish

this is a story of rebuke   puke
regeneration of family   re-nig, re-nig

bigness of the minute   livid
indelible as a statute   astute

                                   still

nothing is etched ~~here~~   what's next?
~~~~ erasure   a black hole
of sorts   of sorting

underground
down low   to say the least
under current   newsworthy
undertow   inert

earthen and dirty   mundane
the airing of so much

In a bowel, belly
and womb
                                   in the round
a bowl of balls   around it
and ovaries

blue black in fact
wishing for motion
a fluidity

no rules
but rulers

an abacus
manipulation of digits

an amber text

as one descends
time spent counted

weighted
the inevitable below
bottom

sometimes sunless
and shitty
mire. admixture

decay. composition
end and begun

the familiar
story of him

the finale is already
known but the journey
the road

is where

movements and players
characterizations

not just him / him / her / him
but us / but us

beaten
no need to rush
this race

i feel a surge of adrenalin
speeding

we have arrived at where
they mate)

are measured in steppes
enmeshed
wrapped up

airing out
comeuppance

a school
a make up

adding up whelps
dexterity

sunlight mixing with night

descendant
down. down

the world
blow. blew

sometimes lit

quicken

creation

familial
hours upon ours

all ready

an ode to it

you are now

played
nations faced

too simple
bludgeoned

beat up
to complete

melatonin
helping sleep

earth and heir

are dimensioned
enfolded

alternate ending for overview

{after "...bottom"}

sometimes sunless ah, shit!	but sometimes lit
familiar story of his's	familial
	hours up on ours
the finale is already but the road	all ready
	this ode to it
is where	
	you are now.
	Too simple
but us, it's us	us, us
no need to rush this race	to complete, compete race
I just wanna testify	I just wanna testify
a surge of adrenaline	my melatonin
my speed	helps me sleep
we have arrived	
where	
they	earth, the heirs
mete	
	step, mesh

O-ooooooo-oh,

Rapt. Up.

1. <u>1st African encounter: not envy, wonder</u>
green was the color
of my first impression surprised at all that life.

2. <u>A prism: Seeing the light, their hearts</u>
enveloped by dark,
I recall science. It's what's
bounced back, not what is.

3. <u>A misunderstood color</u>
Don't presume the worst.
It's not heat, it's cooling. It's
not anger, a sunset

4. <u>Unless you just mean 'Asians'</u>
How can sallow looks
be what 'yellow' means? I'm too
weak to be afraid.

5. <u>Now that the South is free</u>
I can adorn. Glints,
a peace of sun instead of
ringing irony.

6. <u>Makes Sense</u>
Blending reds and blues
is right. Felling blood and pain
should make one royal.

7. <u>A brown one, not a blue one</u>
Composed by many
things I embrace. And one note
sticks out from the page.

8. <u>The Current Color</u>
Drawn to what I like
Can a deer stop the headlights?
Power is blinding.

18. <u>Sunshine Child (for Fatou)</u>
Delight in the light
bright of the light, delightful
Delight in the light

19. <u>For Osayin: A Cover Up</u>
Grass is green a screen
Trees have green a screen which means
Beings needing green.

20. <u>Better not to understand, but to deal with</u>
But why the white, why?
The white way, way white, way,
weigh, weigh, weighty, white.

21. <u>Do You?</u>
Hoodoo 'oman, no
a hoodoo girl. Hoodoo wo-
man know her hoodoo....

How does it relate to Drumming solo ·

something happened !
a retest or me or anyone
any body

Moussa short text reads from book

One time I was buying something for my daughters.
Some toys. It was pretty early but not terribly so.
I wanted to get it out of the way. You know how
children are.

It was balmy out. Neither hot nor breezy enough to
give you goosebumps. Average.

Something hit me so hard, I thought it was a good
idea.

Rock of Gibraltar.

Actually, it was harder than that. A quasar would be
closer. Everything got blurry from the back.

I woke up shivering I remember. Maybe making
shiva. The wind wasn't knocked out of my chest. My
lungs were. A black hole. What I thought a vision
was something very solid, but diffused to me.

I wanted it to be vague. I wanted not to see.

Haiku

for minuet 1

we are in arms, art
sujugated center crux
of empty. Pregnant.

Haiku

Haiku 2

· Rose completely
          Bloomed

· After or purpose one by
one petals, curl, fall

* Transition b/w Mvmt Crime
or During crime

AFTERWORD

(of)

a book

        a journey

                a dance

                              I   b e g i n   a t   t h e   e n d

The dance entitled *Geography* was conceived, choreographed, and directed by New York–based postmodern choreographer Ralph Lemon. *Geography* premiered October 28, 1997, at the Yale Repertory Theatre, then made a national tour until closing in December at the Brooklyn Academy of Music in New York.

The dance ends with a story. There is other spoken and sung text in *Geography*, but it is never narrative. Like the whole of the dance, the spoken text, when in English, is poetically abstract and nonlinear. When in dialects from the Côte d'Ivoire, the spoken text presumably reads as melody and rhythm to its English-speaking audience.

So when we are told a story in English at the end of an hour and a half, it stands out as an event of clarity and drama. The story is told by Moussa Diabaté, a griot from Guinea who now lives in Brooklyn. He stands very still and glowing in a pitch-black void, speaking to what appears as an empty stage space, and then circles it in a series of careening jumps. The story he tells is metaphorical, about the moment of diaspora, the kidnapping of a man such as this West African for the slave trade.

This illicit journey is described as blurry, black, and confusing. With something to see.

The theater is a place to see. *Geography*, by way of the fact and the trope of diaspora, is an attempt to re-map the theater and what it makes visible. *Geography* takes its place alongside other great texts about late-twentieth-century African-American culture, such as Alvin Ailey's *Revelations* and Bill T. Jones's *Last Supper at Uncle Tom's Cabin/The Promised Land*. Lemon's project, however, goes beyond either celebrating or deconstructing the African slave experience. *Geography*, in the end, is about space, just as its title announces. It's about the space that marks identity and that is marked by journeys, and in particular by the African diaspora. And it's about ritually transforming stage space from the secular to the sacred.

The fundamental irony of dance history is that
the dances that get inscribed—
on celluloid, on magnetic tape, on paper—
are the ones that become real.

Geography is as much a book as it is a dance.
Really, Geography *is an autobiography.*

Not quite the melodrama of Duncan's My Life
Or the soap opera of Gelsey Kirkland's Dancing on My Grave.
A tragedy instead, Greek.
Who is the hero, and what of his fatal flaw?
Who will be stoned in the town square?

What hubris does the artist assume when he decides to tell his/story?
Powerful posture, confused gait.

I.

For Lemon, *Geography* is a trip into unknown territory. Acclaimed as a formalist, downtown choreographer, he was uninterested in any content, let alone racial content, for most of the decade he spent directing his company. He acknowledges that his past work has been "Eurocentric." Only a few members of his company over the years were African American.

With *Geography*, the cast is all black. He chose to work with four dancers and two drummers from the Ivory Coast, one Guinean griot, and an African-American "house" dancer from Richmond, Virginia.

For Lemon, these performers represented a range of locations on the diasporic route between Africa and America, and they provided him with the means to undertake a full-scale inquiry into his own racial identity. "Mirrors of my black self," he called them. Their ambitious collaboration charted the labyrinthine geography of Lemon's long-denied and still ambivalent relationship to African and African-American cultures.

For a year and a half, Lemon undertook what amounts to a performance ethnography. He conducted his fieldwork in the American dance studio, where he staged a cultural, personal, and esthetic encounter between himself and a handpicked group of West African performers. It is this encounter, this space in between two cultures, that *Geography* addresses.

Geography was loosely structured after the *Oresteia*. It obliquely sketches the journey of a figure Lemon conceived of as "James Brown-meets-Orestes." It begins with an introductory section called "Map," continues with "Crime" and "Trial," and then culminates in "Divination." Lemon portrays the exiled son of his mother Africa. Dancing is his crime, a stoning his trial, and an ancestral chorus his threshold to the future.

While this story provided the conceptual framework for the piece, in performance *Geography* is a dense work that defies such causal logic. I've heard the dance criticized for needing editing, and for needing better cues as to when spectators should or should not applaud, given the very different role of the audience in American and African dance practices.

II.

Djédjé stands magnificently atop a tall ladder—
calling out, calling forth from the mountaintop—
as a tinkling glass-bottle curtain lowers behind him, a setting sun, a veil of tears.
He is so solid, and rooted so deeply.

That's what they all are. Each a tree.

When the Africans dance, I hear their feet
padding and pounding the floor.
Ralph slips by soundlessly.

Ralph is fascinated with trance.
Initially, he fumbles in his effort to elicit the altered state.
Too dangerous, he is told. But they could fake it.

In the end, he achieves his own kind of rapture.
Divination
Benediction
Consecration

II.

To require that *Geography* conform to existing laws of genre and culture is to exert exactly that pressure the dance is resisting. *Geography* literally lays bare the space of the stage, revealing the fire wall and the wings. We see the performers who stroll around at the edges of the stage when not in action. As soon as they finish their phrases, they resume their offstage manner. They enter and exit and position props with everyday matter-of-factness. The boundary between onstage and offstage is emphasized so as to be questioned.

But at the same time, the space is highly theatricalized and filled with symbolic references. Rumpled linen suits, straw hats, and a lazily turning ceiling fan, mottled shadows of moonlight through the trees and the gentle cries of crickets (did I just imagine them?) suggest a sweltering evening. Everything is converted into space—lighting, movement, even singing is manipulated for its ability to describe the space between here and there, the space between call and response, and the space between inside the body and out. Silence, too, affects the size and density of the stage.

Space is the medium of exchange between dancers, between cultures, between performer and audience, between secular and sacred.

III.

Who does Ralph want to be?
Emerson or Ellison.
James Brown. A Temptation.
A griot. A god. An underworld informant.
Or, rather. Where does Ralph want to be?
Have body, will travel.

The question is no longer: what is dance.
The question is: what does dance do.
When these African dancers look into your face,
You may fall out of your seat.

III.

The dance begins with a ritual exchange between two spectral figures dressed in ancestral gauze gowns, who will reappear toward the end of the piece when an apotheosis restores us to the moment of origin, the story of diaspora. The ritual exchange that begins it all is the discovery of rhythm, in the form of a rock banged against the earth. When another man approaches the first, the gift of rhythm is bestowed upon him, and the rock and roll chant of James Brown cues the dancers, who burst onto the stage and as quickly depart. Such eruptions, disruptions, interruptions, disappearances that produce rather than erase new appearances, dispersals, and displacements are the condition of this dance, which embodies the condition of diasporic culture.

Exchange, or dialogue, was the material project of Geography. How do two sets of bodies, constructed and practiced so differently, create a single dance?

Lemon tried to inhabit the Africans' way of moving while recognizing that goal as an impossibility. As he explained it, "You can never really give up your own culture, but you have to surrender to the situation." He recalled being labeled "white" in Ghana, because he is not from Africa.

Refusing simply to blend the two vocabularies or compose an obvious turn-taking structure, Lemon chose instead to use as his material the very contradictions, tensions, and discrepancies that arose during his intercultural experiment.

Lemon's postmodern movement style is individual, silent, light, supple, free-flowing, and internally focused. The West Africans' style is communal, theatrical, strong, grounded, rhythmic, structured, and externally directed. Lemon's sense of space is geometric, and theirs is organic. He dances secular energy; they dance religious spirit. His knees give out after sixteen counts of their dancing, and their hips resist opening out for his. Where his feet stretch, theirs flex.

To make the creative process as mutual as possible, Lemon devised a workshop method that began with the dancers' own movement material, itself an amalgam of their pan-African performance troupes at home, and cycled it through a series of improvisations. In short: the dancers responded to videotapes of themselves responding to Lemon responding to them. To further the fracturing, he asked them to manipulate their movement—to retrograde it, for example, or perform it without using the arms. The drummers and dancers worked out the counts for the final phrase, which Lemon continued to tweak. At the end of these extended exchanges, the dancers remained themselves, only turned inside out. And Lemon had so incorporated the eruptive energy of his collaborators that in his central solo he actually managed to implode—without destroying—his own loping, looping movement.

IV.

I've never observed someone so fearful and fearless at the same time.
(Ralph realized immediately the price of passage.)

Geography *plots a disorienting route,*
not because it traverses such distance
as fatigues the limbs
but because it fathoms such depth
as unhinges the equilibrium.

IV.

As important as the movement is the mise-en-scène. The set, by installation artist Nari Ward, is an environment of urban detritus but with a mythical patina. And its shadows limn a shifting landscape. Filling this deliberately low-tech space is a highly textured soundscape: West African singing and drumming, poetic text by Tracie Morris, electro-acoustic music by Francisco López, a sensor-triggered contrast of chirping birds and blasting alarms by Paul D. Miller; and always the sound of feet, which patter as expressively as the tongue.

And the spoken text situates the real and mythical place as well, referring to heaven and hell and to the womb, and to a dead garden.

Lemon choreographed not so much a dance as an environment that hosts an interlocking series of interactions. *Geography* is structured like its front curtain of embroidered mattress springs, which functions as screen and frame and fence and cage. It is like the backdrop of glass bottles. The bottle and mattress spring curtains are fragile quilts of everyday objects made sparkling and beautiful. They are artifactual shards of a life unseen, which fit together like the drums onstage, each contributing its own to the fabric of the whole.

And violence is a part of that fabric. What starts out as the minuet transforms into hand-to-hand combat. The veneer of civilization reveals its violent underbelly.

The rocks reappear, this time for use in a ritual stoning.

But the ancestral figures reappear, too, and the stage is then transfigured. Very slowly the curtain of glinting, tinkling, jewel-like bottles lowers to the floor. And as it lowers, one dancer's voice rings out, reverberates, blesses this place that now fills with white-gowned figures, whose popping, intensifying energy is matched by a howling, hollow sound that grows to engulf them. The movement and sound seem to expand the stage. There are no edges, no boundaries, no borders.

And then Moussa tells his story.

And like the story he tells, *Geography* is blurry, black, and confusing. And it is something to see.

But what's seen is not simply another dance in Lemon's repertoire. He has transfigured the very ground of his practice. *Geography* is, in a sense, a project of recovery and a ritual marking of the stage as a sacred place. By inquiring into the nature of the diasporic journey and his own racial identity, Lemon has asked: How does the body circulate? Sound travels, light travels, energy travels, the body certainly travels. And so does identity. Lemon has reinvented the theater as a place to see more than just the changing shapes and patterns of arms and legs. The stage that the griot addresses may appear to be a pitch-black void, but it is not. The space is filled with ancestors telling their stories.

Ann Daly

ACKNOWLEDGMENTS

Special Thanks to:

Rina Drucker and Root Group. Ann Rosenthal, Jenny Tool and MAPP. Stan Wojewodski Jr., Victoria Nolan, Mark Bly, Ben Sammler, Rich Gold, Jenny Friend, Katherine Profeta, Peter Novak, Carla Jackson and the staff of Yale Repertory Theatre.

Akpa Yves Didier "James," Djeli Moussa Diabaté, Orida Diabaté, Carlos Funn, Djédjé Djédjé Gervais, Kouakou Yao "Angelo," Goulei Tchepoho, Zaoli Mabo Tapé, Nai Zou. Souleymane Koly and Werewere Liking for making these artists available.

Tracie Morris, Nari Ward, Francisco Lopez, Paul D. Miller, Stan Pressner, Liz Prince, Rob Gorton, an unforgettable collaboration.

Sam Miller and Cynthia Mayeda, who introduced the landscape. Mikki Shepard and Maurine Knighton for getting me to Africa and bringing the Africans to America. Polly Motley and Molly Davies for the Vermont retreat.

Stephanie French, Karen Brosius, Marilynn Donini, Jennifer Goodale, Marcia Sullivan for their ongoing support.

Elissa Bernstein, Jack Kupferman, Norton Owen, Baraka Sele, Stanley Smith, Marcia Sullivan for being board members for so long.

Pam and Judd Weisberg for the trees. T. Charles Erickson for the photographs. Olga Garay for getting me to Haiti, the beginning. Zao, Oswald, and DañEl Diaz for the guidance.

Michael Dinwiddie for reminding me to write it all down. K for her boundless love. Chelsea for staying close by. Ruth and Ralph and the Lemon family for the unflinching support.

CONTENTS

ABOUT THE AUTHORS

RALPH LEMON formed the Ralph Lemon Company in 1985, which for ten years performed as a touring dance ensemble, receiving numerous residencies, commissions, and grants as well as critical and popular acclaim. In 1995, Lemon disbanded his touring company and rededicated his organization, Cross Performance Inc., to the creation of new forms of performance and presentation. Among the projects currently available are *Persephone*, published by Wesleyan University Press, which includes photographs by Philip Trager, poems by Rita Dove and Eavan Boland, and text by Lemon and Andrew Szegedy-Maszak; *Konbit*, a video documentary collage about the Haitan community in Miami; and *Three*, a film created by Lemon, Bebe Miller, and Isaac Julien. Lemon is currently working on *The Geography Trilogy*, three full-evening performance works created over a six-year span (1996–2002) that investigate an apparent collision of cultures and a search for personal and artistic identity within a broader world arena. In 1999, Lemon was honored with a CalArts Alpert Award in the Arts and was invited to be a participant in the National Theatre Artist Residency Program, administered by Theatre Communications Group, the national organization for the American theater, and funded by The Pew Charitable Trusts. Presently, Lemon is an Associate Artist at Yale Repertory Theatre.

ANN DALY is Associate Professor of Dance History/Criticism at The University of Texas at Austin. She has written on dance and culture for publications including *American Studies*, *Dance Research Journal*, *Dance Theater Journal*, *Performing Arts Journal*, *Village Voice*, and *Women & Performance*. Former president of the Dance Critics Association, she is a contributor to the *New York Times* Arts & Leisure section and contributing editor to *TDR: A Journal of Performance Studies*. Her book *Done into Dance: Isadora Duncan in America* was awarded the 1996 Congress On Research in Dance Award for Outstanding Publication. Her book-in-progress is entitled "When Writing Becomes Gesture."

TRACIE MORRIS is a multimedia performance poet who has worked in theater, dance, music, and film. Her poetry has been anthologized in literary magazines, newspapers, and books, including *360 Degrees: A Revolution of Black Poets, Listen Up!, Aloud: Voices from the Nuyorican Poets Cafe*, and *Soul*. Her words have also been featured in pieces commissioned by Aaron Davis Hall, the International Festival for the Arts, The Kitchen, and Yale Repertory Theater. Ms. Morris has received numerous awards for poetry, including the New York Foundation for the Arts Fellowship, Creative Capital Fellowship, The National Haiku Slam Championship in 1993, and an Asian Cultural Council Fellowship. She is the author of two poetry collections, *Intermission* and *Chap-T-her Won*. In addition to being a working artist, Ms. Morris is guest faculty of Performance Poetry at Sarah Lawrence College.